New York State

The Militia Law of the State of New York

Passed April 23, 1862

New York State

The Militia Law of the State of New York
Passed April 23, 1862

ISBN/EAN: 9783337812904

Printed in Europe, USA, Canada, Australia, Japan

Cover: Foto ©ninafisch / pixelio.de

More available books at **www.hansebooks.com**

THE
MILITIA LAW

OF THE

STATE OF NEW YORK.

1862.

ALBANY:
WEED, PARSONS AND COMPANY, PRINTERS.
1862.

THE MILITIA LAW.

Chapter 477.

AN ACT to provide for the enrollment of the militia, the organization and discipline of the national guard of the State of New York, and for the public defence.

Passed April 23, 1862; by a two-third vote.

The People of the State of New York, represented in Senate and Assembly, do enact as follows:

OF THE PERSONS SUBJECT TO MILITARY DUTY.

SECTION 1. All able-bodied, white male citizens, between the ages of eighteen and forty-five years, residing in this state and not exempted by the laws of the United States, shall be subject to military duty, excepting: {Persons subject to military duty.}

1st. All persons in the army or navy or volunteer force of the United States.

2d. Ministers and preachers of the gospel.

3d. The lieutenant-governor, members and officers of the legislature, the secretary of state, attorney-general, comptroller, state engineer and surveyor, state treasurer, and clerks and employees in their offices, judicial officers of this state, including justices of the peace, sheriffs, coroners and constables.

4th. Persons being of the people called Shakers or Quakers, professors, teachers and students in all colleges, and professors, teachers and students in the several academies and common schools.

5th. Persons who have been or hereafter shall be regularly and honorably discharged from the army or navy of the United States, in consequence of the performance of military duty, in pursuance of any law of this state, and such firemen as are now exempted by law.

6th. The commissioned officers who shall have served as such in the militia of this state, or in any one of the United States, for the space of seven years; but no officer shall be so exempt unless by his resignation after such term of service duly accepted, or in some other lawful manner, he shall have been honorably discharged.

7th. Every non-commissioned officer, musician and private, of every uniform company or troop raised or hereafter to be raised, who has or shall hereafter uniform himself according to the provisions of any law of this state, and who shall have performed service in such company or troop for the space of seven years from the time of his enrollment therein, shall be exempt from military duty, except in cases of war, insurrection or invasion.

Time of service, how computed.

§ 2. If any member of such company or troop, who shall have been regularly uniformed and equipped, shall, upon his removal out of the beat of such company or troop, or upon the disbandment thereof, enlist into any other uniform company or troop, and uniform and equip himself therefor, and serve in the same, whenever the whole time of his service in such companies or troops, computed together, shall amount to seven years, he shall be exempt from military duty in like manner as if he had served for the whole period in the company or troop in which he was first enrolled.

§ 3. Idiots, lunatics, paupers, habitual drunkards, and persons convicted of infamous crimes, shall not be subject to military duty.

OF THE ENROLLMENT OF PERSONS SUBJECT TO MILITARY DUTY.

Enrollment.

§ 4. Under the direction and superintendence of the commander-in-chief, all persons liable to military duty within this state, who are not already members of the organized militia thereof, shall, immediately upon the passage of this act, and from time to time thereafter, as the commander-in-chief shall deem necessary, but as often as once in every two years, be enrolled by the captain or commandant of the company district within whose bounds such person shall reside, or if there be no such captain or commandant, then by an officer to be detailed by the commanding officer of the regiment in which such company district is situated, or to be appointed by the commander-in-chief. Such enrollment shall distinctly specify the names and residences of the persons enrolled, and shall also divide the same into two classes, the persons between the ages of eighteen and thirty years to constitute one class, and the persons between the ages of thirty and forty-five years to constitute the other class; four copies of such enrollment shall be prepared by the officer making the same, one of which, after the same shall have been corrected as hereinafter provided, shall be retained by him, another shall be filed in the office of the town or city clerk in which such company district is situated, if there be such office, another shall be filed in the office of the clerk of the county where such district is situated, and the fourth shall be filed in the adjutant-general's office; the officer making such enrollment may, with the approval of the commander-in-chief, appoint one or more of his non-commissioned officers, or other proper persons, to assist in making said enrollment and copying said rolls; the persons making such enrollment shall be compensated at the rate of one dollar and fifty cents per day for every day necessarily spent in making and copying the same; the number of days to be certified by the commandant of the regiment, and not to exceed ten, and the amount of such compensation to be paid by the comptroller upon production of such certificate, together with the certificates of the town clerk, county clerk and adjutant-general, that such rolls have been duly filed in their offices. Such rolls shall be so filed on or before the first day of July in each year in which such enrollment shall be made.

§ 5. For the purpose of preparing such enrollment, the assessors in each city, village, town or ward of this state, shall allow captains or commandants of companies or other officers appointed for that purpose, as above provided, at all proper times to examine their assessment rolls and to take copies thereof, and the clerks of all towns and cities shall in like manner, at all proper times, allow the said commandant or other officer to examine and copy the poll lists on file in their offices. <small>Assessors and clerks to allow enrolling officers to examine assessment rolls and poll lists.</small>

§ 6. All tavern keepers, keepers of boarding houses, persons having boarders in their families, and any master and mistress of any dwelling house, shall, upon the application of any officer authorized to make such enrollment, <small>Information of persons liable to be enrolled.</small>

give information of the names of all persons residing or lodging in such house, liable to be enrolled, and all other proper information concerning such persons as such officer may demand.

Penalty for not giving information of persons liable to enrollment.
§ 7. If any person of whom information is required by any such officer, in order to enable him to comply with the provisions of this act, shall refuse to give such information, or shall give false information, he shall forfeit and pay ten dollars for each item of information demanded of him by any such officer and falsely stated, and the like sum for each individual name that may be refused, concealed or falsely stated; and every person who shall refuse to give his own name and proper information, when applied to by any such officer, or shall give a false name or information, shall forfeit and pay a like sum; such penalties to be recovered in any court of competent jurisdiction, in the name of the People of the State of New York; and it is hereby made the duty of such officer to report the names of all persons who may incur any penalty in this section prescribed, to the commandant of the regimental district in which they reside.

Enrollment to be copied and filed.
§ 8. Whenever an enrollment shall be made as provided in this act, the clerk of the board of supervisors of each county shall cause to be published, once a week for four weeks previous to the first day of August, in a newspaper published in such county, a notice that such rolls have been completed and filed as aforesaid, which notice shall also specify that any person who claims that he is, for any reason, exempt from military duty, shall, on or before the fifteenth day of August, then next ensuing, file a written statement of such exemption, verified by affidavit, in the office of said town or city clerk, or of the county clerk, if there be no such town or city clerk, and the publication of such notice, shall be a sufficient notice of such enrollment to all persons named therein; such roll shall be made in the form prescribed by the commander-in-chief, and the adjutant-general shall furnish to all commandants of companies, suitable blanks and instructions therefor.

Foreman of fire companies to deliver lists of their members.
§ 9. Such commandant shall not include in such enrollment the names of any officers nor members of the uniformed militia of this state, nor of the officers or members of any fire company, and the foreman of every fire com-

pany in any city, village or town of this state, shall, before the fifteenth day of May in each year, file in the office of the town or city clerk, a list containing the names of all persons belonging to their respective companies, which list shall show the town or ward in which each member of such company resides.

§ 10. All persons claiming exemptions shall file a written statement of the same, verified by affidavit, in the office of the town or city clerk, or of the county clerk, in case there be no such town or city clerk, on or before the fifteenth day of August, in default of which such person shall lose the benefit of such exemption, except such as are especially exempt by act of Congress. *Exemption statement to be filed.*

§ 11. The captain, commandant, or other officer making such enrollment, shall thereupon, if such person be exempt, according to law, mark the word "exempt" opposite the name of each person presenting such exemption; if such exemption be permanent, the name of such person shall not be included in any subsequent enrollment. If any person shall swear falsely in such affidavit, he shall be guilty of perjury. *Exemption to be noted.*

§ 12. The persons thus enrolled shall form the reserve militia of the State of New York; those between the ages of eighteen and thirty years shall constitute the reserve of the first class, and those between the ages of thirty and forty-five years shall constitute the reserve of the second class. *Reserve militia reserve of the first and second classes.*

§ 13. The reserve militia of the first and second classes, except such as shall volunteer, or be drafted as members of the national guard as hereinafter provided, shall assemble in their several company districts armed and equipped, as provided by law, for parade and inspection, on the first Monday of September in each year, at such hour and place as the captain or commandant shall designate in orders to be posted in three public places in the said company district for ten days, and shall be under the orders of the captain or commandant of such district, and such captain or commandant shall make a roster of all such as shall attend at such parade, armed and equipped as aforesaid, and shall file a copy of the same on or before the tenth day of October, in the office of the adjutant-general and of the county clerk. *Yearly parade and inspection of the reserve militia.*

THE MILITIA LAW

Fine for non-attendance at parade.

§ 14. All persons duly enrolled as aforesaid, who shall neglect to attend said parade, shall be subject to a fine of one dollar, which, if not paid to the county treasurer on or before the first day of December, shall be collected by the collector or receiver of taxes of the town or city in which said company district is situated, and the supervisors of the several counties at their annual meetings are authorized and directed to annex a list of the several delinquents with the fines set opposite their respective names to the assessment rolls of the several towns and wards, and the warrants for the collection of the same, shall direct the collectors and receivers of taxes to collect the amount from every person appearing by the said assessment roll liable to pay the same, in the same manner as taxes are collected. The same to be paid to the county treasurer, and when the name of any person, between the ages of eighteen and twenty-one years, shall appear on the said roll liable to pay the said fine, the said warrant shall direct the collector to collect the same of the father, master or guardian with whom such person shall reside, or out of any property such minor may have in the city, village, town, or ward, and such collector shall proceed and execute such warrant, and no property now exempt from execution shall be exempt from the payment of such fine.

County treasurer to pay to comptroller one dollar for each delinquent, to borrow money on credit of county to meet comptroller's order for the same. Supervisors to raise amount by taxation.

§ 15. The county treasurer of each county shall, on or before the fifteenth day of March in each year, pay to the comptroller upon his order the sum of one dollar for each person so enrolled who does not appear from said roster to have attended such parade. And in case he shall not, on the presentation of such draft, have received all or any of the money directed by this act to be collected and paid to him, he is hereby authorized and directed to borrow an amount sufficient to pay said draft upon the credit of the county, and the sum borrowed shall be a county charge, to be assessed by the board of supervisors of said county at their next annual meeting, upon the taxable property of said county, and collected as other county assessments shall be assessed and collected. And it shall be the duty of the county treasurers of the several counties, and the commanding officers of the several regiments, to report and certify under oath to the board of supervisors at their annual meetings the deficiencies arising from the non-collection of military fines, within their respective counties and regimental districts.

§ 16. The provisions of article first, title three, chapter thirteen, of part first of the Revised Statutes, shall apply to this act so far as the same are applicable. *Certain provisions of Revised Statutes to apply.*

§ 17. The bond required to be executed by the collector, receiver of taxes and county treasurer shall apply to any moneys required to be collected for military purposes by this act. *Bonds of collectors, &c., and county treasurer to apply to this act.*

§ 18. Any deficiency arising from the non-collection of said fines shall be a county charge, and shall be raised as aforesaid by the supervisors of said county by taxation on the real and personal estates therein in the manner now provided by law. *Deficiency, how raised by supervisors.*

§ 19. If any collector or receiver of taxes, county treasurer, town, county, or city clerk, or supervisor, or any other civil or military officer, charged with any duty under the provisions of this act, shall refuse or neglect to perform any of the duties required of him by this act, he shall forfeit and pay the sum of not less than twenty-five nor more than one hundred dollars for each and every offense, to be recovered in the name of the people of the State of New York, and if any of such officers shall willfully neglect or refuse to perform such duties as are hereby required, he shall be deemed guilty of a misdemeanor, and it shall be the duty of the district attorney of any county within which such delinquent offender resides, upon the complaint of the commanding officer of the regiment, to prosecute the same. Any penalty incurred and paid or collected under this section shall be paid into the treasury of the county and belong to the military fund of such regiment. *Penalty in case certain officers refuse to act.*

OF THE GENERAL ORGANIZATION OF THE MILITIA, AND THE ORGANIZATION OF THE NATIONAL GUARD OF THE STATE OF NEW YORK.

Of Organization.

§ 20. The commander-in-chief of the militia of this state shall organize and arrange the same, and the districts therefor, into divisions, brigades, regiments, battalions, squadrons, troops, batteries and companies, and cause the same to be numbered as nearly in conformity to the laws of the United States as local circumstances and the public convenience *Divisions, brigades, regiments, &c., how organized, changed, consolidated, &c.*

may permit, and may alter, divide, annex or consolidate the same and the districts thereof, and dismiss supernumerary officers, who were made such by an excess of officers of equal grade being thrown into any division, brigade, regimental or company district. The present divisions, brigades, regiments, battalions, troops, squadrons, batteries and companies, and the districts thereof, shall remain as now established by law, subject to the power of the commander-in-chief, to alter, divide, annex or consolidate the same as above set forth. Regimental districts, except in cities, shall conform, as nearly as convenient, to the assembly districts of this state.

The National Guard of the State of New York.

§ 21. The organized militia of this state shall be known as "the National Guard of the State of New York," and shall consist of eight divisions, thirty-two brigades, and one hundred and twenty-eight regiments and battalions, and such batteries, troops, or squadrons as may be formed in pursuance of the provisions of this act, but nothing herein contained shall be so construed as to interfere with the power of the commander-in-chief, in case of war or insurrection, or of imminent danger thereof, to make further drafts of the militia, and to form new regiments, battalions, brigades, or divisions and districts therefor.

Uniformed militia to form part of the national guard.

§ 22. The national guard shall include the present uniformed militia of this state, and such volunteers as shall enroll themselves therein in the several districts of this state, and such persons as may be drafted therein, as hereinafter provided, and shall be organized, and shall serve as engineers, artillery, light artillery, cavalry, infantry and rifles, as the commander-in-chief shall direct.

Officers to be appointed in the first instance in unorganized districts.

§ 23. The commander-in-chief is hereby authorized and empowered, so soon as may be convenient after the passage of this act, to appoint and commission the brigade, regimental and company officers, in the first instance, necessary to complete the organization of all military districts hereafter to be created, and to fill all vacancies necessary for the complete organization of all military districts now created in this state, but not sufficiently organized for an election. All officers superseded by such appointment shall become supernumerary officers.

Non-commissioned officers to be ap-

§ 24. The commandant of each regimental district, for the purpose of organization, is hereby authorized and required to appoint the non-commissioned officers required by law for each company in his district, and to issue to such non-commissioned officers the proper warrants of their appointment, until the organization of such regiment shall be complete. *(pointed in unorganized regiments.)*

§ 25. The organization of the national guard shall conform to the provisions of the laws of the United States, and their system of discipline and exercise shall conform as nearly as may be to that of the army of the United States, as it now is, or may hereafter be prescribed by congress. *(Organization to conform to laws of U. S.)*

§ 26. Company officers shall use their best efforts to obtain sufficient volunteers to raise their respective companies to the number of at least thirty-two non-commissioned officers and privates, which number is hereby fixed as the minimum, and one hundred as the maximum of such company organizations. *(Minimum and maximum numbers of company organizations.)*

§ 27. In case any company of the national guard shall not, on or before the first day of October next, by voluntary enlistments, reach the minimum number of thirty-two non-commissioned officers and privates, or in case such company shall at any time fall below such minimum, or in case a sufficient number of persons shall not volunteer to organize new companies in the unorganized company districts, it shall be lawful for the commander-in-chief to order a sufficient number of persons to be drafted from the reserve militia of the first class, in the manner hereinafter provided, to raise such company to, and maintain the same at, such minimum number. The persons so drafted shall thereupon be enrolled as members of said company, and, unless they shall find substitutes, as hereinafter provided, shall be subject to the duties herein mentioned, and in case of non-performance of such duties, shall be subject to the pains and penalties herein mentioned; and such persons, or their substitutes, shall be entitled to all the privileges and exemptions conferred under any of the terms of this act, provided that no new company shall be organized in time of peace, if thereby the entire force shall exceed thirty thousand officers and men. *(Voluntary enlistments, drafts and substitutes.)* *(National guard limited to 30,000 in time of peace.)*

§ 28. To every company there shall be one captain, one first, one second lieutenant, four sergeants, four corporals and three musicians, except in companies of artillery and *(Company officers.)*

cavalry, which may have one first and two second lieutenants, provided, however, that whenever any company shall exceed fifty rank and file it may have five sergeants and eight corporals.

Companies to be formed in separate company districts when practicable.

§ 29. Companies shall be formed in separate company districts when practicable, but the commander-in-chief may, in his discretion, organize more companies than one in the same district, or parts of a company in different districts.

Divisions, brigades, regiments, how composed.

§ 30. Each division shall consist of not less than two brigades, each brigade not less than two regiments, each regiment of ten battalion companies.

Battalions, batteries, &c., may be organized.

§ 31. The commander-in-chief shall have power to organize, under the provisions of this act, battalions of infantry and rifles, and battalions, batteries or companies of artillery, or for special services where it is not expedient or convenient to form regimental organizations, or whenever the exigency of the service may require.

Men not to leave company to join other companies or fire companies.

§ 32. No non-commissioned officer, musician or private, belonging to any troop of cavalry or company of artillery, light artillery, riflemen or infantry, shall leave the troop or company to which he belongs to serve as a fireman in any fire company now raised or hereafter to be raised in any city or county; nor shall he leave such troop or company and enlist in any other, without the written consent of the commandant of the regiment, battalion or battery, and of the squadron, troop or company to which he belongs, except he shall have removed out of the beat of such troop or company. Such exception shall not apply to any troop or company situate in any of the cities of this state.

Minors not to join without consent unless drafted.

§ 33. No person under the age of twenty-one years, shall hereafter enlist in or join any uniform troop or company, without the consent of his parent or guardian, master or mistress, unless drafted in accordance with the provisions of this act.

Uniforms.

§ 34. Every officer of the line and staff, and every officer and private of any uniform company of this state, shall provide himself, according to the provisions of this act, with a uniform complete, which shall be such as the commander-in-chief shall prescribe, and subject to such restrictions, limitations and alterations as he may order.

§ 35. Any non-commissioned officer or private may, upon his enlistment, or upon being drafted in accordance with the provisions of this act, if he so elect, be furnished at the expense of the state with the proper uniform and equipments of his regiment or corps; in such case an entry, to that effect, shall be made upon the company roll, and such uniform shall be furnished by the quarter master-general's department, upon the requisition of the commandant of the company, countersigned by the commandant of the regiment or battalion; but such uniform and equipments shall in no case be different from those prescribed by the general regulations for the military forces of the State of New York, unless by special authority of the commander-in-chief.

Uniforms in what cases furnished by the state.

§ 36. In case such uniform and equipments be furnished in accordance with the last preceding section, the same shall be left at the company armory for safe keeping, and the person applying for the same shall be charged with the value thereof, and shall be entitled to receive half pay only for services under this act, at drills, parades, encampments and lake and sea coast defence duty, until the sum charged against him therefor shall have been liquidated by such service, when such uniform and equipment shall become the property of such person.

Uniforms to be left at armory.

§ 37. Whoever shall presume to sell or dispose of such uniform or equipments, or to secrete or remove the same with intent to sell or dispose thereof, before the same shall become his property by such service as aforesaid, shall be deemed guilty of a misdemeanor, and shall be punished by imprisonment in a county jail for not less than two nor more than six months, or by a fine of not more than two hundred and fifty dollars nor less than fifty dollars, or by both such fine and imprisonment.

Penalty if uniform be removed or secreted.

§ 38. The quartermaster-general shall, under the direction and with the approval of the commander-in-chief, cause to be manufactured in the several regimental districts of this state, the uniforms and equipments, which may, from time to time be required for each regiment for the purposes mentioned in this act. And the comptroller, upon the order of the commander-in-chief, shall draw his warrant upon the treasurer for such sums as shall, from time to time, be expended for the purchase or manufacture of said

Quartermaster-general to cause uniforms and equipments to be manufactured.

uniforms and equipments: Provided, always, that the price paid for the same shall, in no case, exceed the prices established by the general regulations for the army of the United States for articles of like description.

Accounts to be audited.

§ 39. All vouchers and accounts under the last preceding section shall, from time to time, be audited by a committee, to consist of the comptroller, treasurer, and secretary of state.

Books to be provided.

§ 40. The commander-in-chief shall, from time to time, direct such books, as to him shall appear expedient, as a guide for the military forces of this state, to be provided, and shall furnish the same to all commissioned officers at the expense of the state.

Divisions, &c., to be numbered.

§ 41. The commander-in-chief shall cause each company, squadron, troop, battery, battalion, regiment, brigade, and division to be numbered or lettered in such manner as he shall deem proper and best calculated to secure uniformity. Each company, squadron, troop, battery, battalion, regiment, brigade and division shall be known by its number and designation, which shall be registered at the adjutant-general's office.

Non-commissioned officers, how chosen. Commissioned officers in cities, when deemed within bounds of command.

§ 42. Non-commissioned officers shall be chosen from the members of the company to which they belong. All commissioned officers residing in any city or incorporated village in this state shall be deemed to be within the bounds of their respective commands, providing any part of the military district to which they properly belong shall be located within such city or village.

Existing uniformed companies to be deemed organized under this act.

§ 43. All existing uniformed companies, in any such regimental district, city or village, shall be deemed to be organized under the provisions of this act; but no such company shall be so constituted, unless at the time of such application it contains thirty-two non-commissioned officers and privates.

Election for field officers when to be held.

§ 44. Whenever six uniformed companies shall be organized in any of the regimental districts of this state, the commander-in-chief shall order an election to be held for the choice of suitable persons to fill the offices of colonel, lieutenant-colonel and major, in such regiment, by directing some suitable officer to give the proper notices of such election, and to preside thereat, unless such officers shall already have been elected or appointed.

§ 45. As soon as the field officers in the regiments in any of the brigade districts of this state shall be duly chosen and commissioned, the commander-in-chief shall order an election to be held for the choice of a suitable person to fill the office of brigadier-general and brigade inspector in such brigade district, by directing some suitable officer to give the proper notices of such election and preside thereat, unless such brigadier-general and brigade inspector shall already have been elected or appointed as provided by this act. *Election for brigadier-general and brigade inspector, when to be held.*

§ 46. All commissioned officers rendered supernumerary by the provisions of this act, and every officer rendered supernumerary by any consolidation or alteration of regiments, battalions, squadrons, troops or companies, shall be entitled to all the privileges conferred by any preceding law (except command), and shall be exempt from the performance of any military duty, except in cases of war and insurrection, provided they shall, within one year after being so rendered supernumerary, have reported themselves to the adjutant-general as such; provided, however, that no officer rendered supernumerary shall be entitled to vote at any election held for the choice of officers, or serve as a member of any court-martial. *Supernumerary officers.*

§ 47. Volunteers under the provisions of this act may be received in any company of the national guard, whether such volunteer reside in the company district or not; but persons liable to military duty shall be drafted only in the district where they may reside. *Volunteers, how received.*

§ 48. Any officer, non-commissioned officer, musician or uniformed private, who may change his residence from within the bounds of the first division into any adjacent county, or from within any county adjacent into the said division district, shall not thereby vacate his office or post, but he shall be held to duty in the division, brigade, regiment, troop or company to which he was attached at the time of such change of residence, and he shall be subject to duty therein and shall be entitled to all privileges, immunities and exemptions allowed by law, and shall be liable to fines and penalties, and the collection of them, in the same manner as if such change of residence had not taken place; and process for the collection of such fines *Change of residence not to vacate office in certain cases.*

and penalties may be executed in either New York or any adjacent county.

ON THE ELECTION AND APPOINTMENT OF MILITARY OFFICERS, AND THE TENURE OF THEIR OFFICES.

Major-generals and commissary, how appointed.

§ 49. All major-generals, and the commissary-general, shall be nominated by the governor, and appointed by him, with the consent of the senate.

Resolution to be transmitted to adjutant-general.

§ 50. The resolution of the senate, concurring in any nomination made by the governor to a military office, shall be certified by the president and clerk of the senate, and be transmitted to the adjutant-general, who shall issue the commission and record the same in books to be provided by him.

Staff of commander-in-chief.

§ 51. The staff of the commander-in-chief shall consist of the adjutant-general, an inspector-general, engineer-in-chief, judge-advocate-general, quartermaster-general, commissary-general of subsistence, paymaster-general, surgeon-general and three aids, who shall be appointed by the governor, and whose commission shall expire with the time for which the governor shall have been elected.

Commissary-general of ordnance, his oath.

§ 52. The commissary-general shall hereafter be known as the commissary-general of ordnance, and shall not enter on the duties of his office until he shall have taken the oath of office prescribed in the constitution. Such oath shall be taken before any officer authorized to administer the same oath to the attorney-general within the same period, and subject to the same regulations.

Captains and other officers, how chosen.

§ 53. Captains, subalterns, and non-commissioned officers of organized regiments, shall be chosen by the written or printed votes of the members of their respective companies; field officers of organized regiments and battalions, by the written or printed votes of the commissioned officers of their respective regiments and battalions; and brigadier-generals and brigade inspectors, by the written or printed votes of the field officers of their respective brigades, if organized.

Staff officers, how chosen.

§ 54. Major-generals, brigadier-generals, and commanding officers of regiments or battalions, shall appoint the staff officers of their respective divisions, brigades, regiments or battalions, whose term of office shall expire when the persons appointing them shall retire from office; but they shall continue to hold such office until their successors shall be appointed and have qualified.

§ 55. The commissioned officers of the militia shall be commissioned by the governor; and no commissioned officer can be removed from office unless by the senate, on the recommendation of the governor, stating the grounds on which such removal is recommended ; or by the decision of a court-martial, or retiring or examining board, pursuant to law. *Officers, how commissioned and removed.*

§ 56. Sergeant-majors, quartermaster-sergeants, sergeant standard-bearers and drum majors, shall be appointed by the commanding officer of the regiment or battalion to which they shall belong, by warrant under the hand of such commanding officer, and shall hold their offices during his pleasure. *Subordinate officers, how appointed and removed.*

§ 57. Whenever the office of a brigadier-general is vacant in any organized brigade, the commander-in-chief shall issue an order for an election to fill the vacancy, and shall designate a major-general or some other proper officer to preside at such election. *Vacancies in office of brigadier-general.*

§ 58. The officer so designated shall cause a written or printed notice to be served on each of the field officers of the brigade in which the vacancy exists, at least ten days previous to the election, specifying the time and place of holding such election. *Notice of election.*

§ 59. Whenever the office of any field officer in any organized regiment or battalion is vacant, the commanding officer of the brigade to which such regiment or battalion belongs, shall cause a written or printed notice to be served on each commissioned officer in such regiment or battalion of an election to fill the vacancy. The notice shall specify the time and place of holding the election, and be served at least five days before such election shall take place. *Elections to fill vacancy of field officer.*

§ 60. Whenever the office of a captain or subaltern in any organized company or troop is vacant, the commanding officer of the regiment or battalion to which such company or troop belong, shall cause a written or printed notice of an election to fill the vacancy, to be served on the members of such company or troop, at least three days before the election shall take place, and shall specify in such notice the time and place of the election. *Election to fill office of captain or subaltern.*

THE MILITIA LAW

Election notices, how served.
§ 61. All notices for any election shall be served on the persons entitled to vote thereat, in the same manner as non commissioned officers, musicians and privates are warned to attend a parade, as prescribed in section one hundred and thirty-nine of this act.

Return of persons notified.
§ 62. The officer issuing the notice shall designate some proper person or persons to serve the same or to direct such service; and the person so designated shall make a return of the persons notified, and of the manner of the service.

Return, how authenticated.
§ 63. The return, if made by a commissioned officer, shall be authenticated by his certificate on honor; if by a non-commissioned officer, by the oath of the person making such service. The oath may be administered by any magistrate or by the officer issuing the notice.

Election, how conducted.
§ 64. The officer causing the notice to be given for any of the aforesaid elections, shall attend at the time and place of holding such elections; he shall organize the meeting and preside thereat, and may, for sufficient cause, adjourn the same from time to time.

Presiding officer.
§ 65. If the officer causing the notices to be given shall not attend the meeting for the election, the officer of the highest rank present, or in case of an equality of rank between two or more, then such of them as the majority of the electors present shall choose, shall preside at such meeting. And the officer issuing such notices shall cause the proper evidence of service of such notices on all the electors to be delivered to such presiding officer. And at meetings for the election of company officers, the company roll, carefully revised, shall in like manner be delivered with such evidence. And if it shall happen at any election for commissioned officers that legal notice has not been given to all the persons entitled to vote thereat, the presiding officer shall adjourn the meeting, and cause such notice to be given. The presence of a person entitled to vote at any election shall be deemed a waiver of his right to take exception to the want of legal notice.

Polls. Canvass
§ 66. The presiding officer at any election for commissioned officers, shall keep the polls opened at least one hour after the time appointed for holding the same. He shall then publicly canvass the votes received from the electors for the officers to be elected, and shall forthwith declare the result, and give notice to every person elected

of his election. If such person shall not, within ten days after being notified of his election, signify to such officer his acceptance, he shall be considered as declining the office to which he shall have been chosen, and an election shall be held for a new choice.

§ 67. Immediately after the person elected shall have signified his acceptance, the officer who shall have presided at the election shall, in case of the election of a brigadier-general, communicate the same to the commander-in-chief; and in all other cases, if not himself the commanding officer of the brigade, shall certify to such commanding officer the names of the persons duly elected. <small>Certificate of election.</small>

§ 68. If at any election an officer, then in commission, shall be elected to fill a vacancy, and shall accept, the electors present, whether such officer be present or absent, shall proceed to elect a person to fill the place of the officer so promoted, if the officers or persons assembled at such meeting have authority to make the choice. <small>Vacancy caused by election, how filled.</small>

§ 69. The commanding officers of brigades shall transmit the names of persons duly elected and approved, or appointed to offices in their respective brigades, to the commander-in-chief, to the end that commissions may be issued to them. <small>Names of persons elected to be transmitted to commander-in-chief.</small>

§ 70. Every person thinking himself aggrieved by the proceedings of any election for a commissioned officer may appeal, if the election be for a brigadier-general, to the commander-in-chief, and in other cases to the commanding officer of the brigade to which such person belongs. <small>Appeal.</small>

§ 71. The officer appealed to shall have power to administer oaths, and shall hear and determine the appeal; and if in his opinion the proceedings at such election are illegal, he shall declare the election void, and shall order an election to be held without delay for a new choice. <small>Appeal, how determined.</small>

§ 72. Any person concerned may appeal from the decision of the commanding officer of the brigade to the commander-in-chief, who shall hear and determine such appeal, and in case it shall be necessary, order a new election. <small>Appeal to commander-in-chief.</small>

§ 73. The commander-in-chief may make such rules and regulations relative to appeals as he shall deem necessary and proper to give full effect to the provisions of the constitution and of this act. <small>Conduct of appeals</small>

Commissions to be issued by commander-in-chief.

§ 74. The commander-in-chief shall issue commissions to all officers duly elected or appointed in pursuance of the provisions of this act; and every officer duly commissioned shall, within ten days after his commission shall be tendered to him, or within ten days after he shall be personally notified that the same is held in readiness for him, by any superior officer, take and subscribe the oath prescribed in the constitution of this state; and in case of neglect or refusal to take such oath within the time mentioned, he shall be deemed to have resigned said office, and a new election shall be forthwith ordered to fill his place. The neglect or refusal of an officer elect to take such oath shall be no excuse for neglect of duty until another shall be duly commissioned in his place.

Oath of commissioned officers.

§ 75. Every commissioned officer shall take and subscribe such oath before a judge of some court of record in this state, county clerk, commissioner to take affidavits, justice of the peace, or some general or field officer who has previously taken it himself, and who is hereby authorized to administer the same.

Certificate on commission.

§ 76. A certificate of the oath shall be indorsed by the officer administering the same on the commission, and a copy thereof shall be filed in the adjutant-general's office.

No fee for oath.

§ 77. No fee shall be received for administering any such oath, or indorsing such certificate.

Vacancies of non-commissioned officers.

§ 78. Any organized company or troop may, at any meeting thereof, elect non-commissioned officers to fill any vacancy therein.

Election, how conducted.

§ 79. Such election shall be directed and conducted by the commanding officer of such company or troop for the time being, who shall certify the names of the persons elected to the commanding officer of the regiment or battalion to which the company or troop belongs, who shall decide upon the legality of the election, and issue warrants to the persons duly elected.

Special meetings of companies.

§ 80. The commandants of companies or troops may, whenever they deem it necessary, call a special meeting of their respective companies or troops for an election of non-commissioned officers.

Votes necessary to a choice.

§ 81. A majority of the votes of all persons present at an election of brigadier-general shall be necessary to a choice; in all other cases a plurality shall be sufficient.

§ 82. No officer shall be considered out of the service on the tender of his resignation until it shall have been accepted by the commander-in-chief. The commanding officers of brigades shall receive the resignations of such commissioned officers as may resign in their respective brigades, and shall transmit the same to the adjutant-general. Resignations of all other commissioned officers shall be made direct to the commander-in-chief. *Resignations, how made.*

§ 83. No officer shall be permitted to resign his commission who shall be under arrest, or shall be returned to a court martial for any deficiency or delinquency; and no resignation shall be accepted unless the officer tendering the same shall furnish to the adjutant-general satisfactory evidence that he has delivered all moneys in his hands as such officer, and all books and other property of the state in his possession to his next superior or inferior officer, or to the officer authorized by law to receive the same, and that his accounts for money or public property are correct. *Resignations, when not allowed.*

§ 84. In time of war, or when the military forces of this state are in actual service, resignations shall take effect thirty days from the date of the order of acceptance, unless otherwise specially ordered by the commander-in-chief. *Resignations in time of war.*

§ 85. On accepting the resignation of any officer, the commander-in-chief shall cause the necessary notices and orders to be given for an election to fill the vacancy so created, provided, however, that when the military forces of this state shall be in the actual service thereof, or in the service of the United States in time of war, insurrection, invasion or imminent danger thereof, the commander-in-chief shall fill all vacancies of commissioned officers by appointment. *Vacancies, how filled.*

§ 86. Every officer who shall move out of the bounds of his command (unless such removal shall not be beyond the bounds of a city in which such command shall lie in whole or in part), and every officer who shall be absent from his command twelve months without leave of the commanding officer of his brigade, shall be considered as having vacated his office, and a new election shall be held, without delay, to fill the vacancy so created, except as above provided. *Removal from bounds of command.*

§ 87. No person shall be allowed to vote at any election for a commissioned or non-commissioned officer of a com- *Voters, their qualifications.*

THE MILITIA LAW

pany, unless he is an actual member of such company where he shall offer his vote, and liable to do military duty therein.

Challenges. § 88. If any person offering to vote at any election for a commissioned officer of a company, shall be challenged as unqualified by any person entitled to vote thereat, the presiding officer shall declare to the person so challenged the qualifications of an elector.

Oath. § 89. If he shall state himself to be duly qualified, and the challenge shall not be withdrawn, the presiding officer shall then tender to him the following oath :

" You do swear (or affirm) that you are an actual member of the company commanded by   , and that you are liable to do military duty therein."

Commissions. § 90. The commissioned officer who shall receive a commission for any subordinate officer, shall, within thirty days thereafter, give notice thereof to the person entitled to it.

Examining board. § 91. The commander-in-chief is hereby authorized, so often as he may deem that the good of the service requires, to appoint a military board or commission of not less than three nor more than five officers, to sit at such place as he shall direct, whose duty it shall be to examine into the physical ability, moral character, capacity, attainments, general fitness for the service, and efficiency of such commissioned officers, as the commander-in-chief may order to be examined by said board, or who may be reported for examination to the adjutant-general by colonels of their regiments, or general officers commanding their brigades or divisions, and upon such report may be ordered to be examined by the commander-in-chief. If the decision of said board be unfavorable to such officer, and be approved by the commander-in-chief, the commission of such officer shall be vacated; provided, always, that no officer shall be eligible to sit on such board or commission whose rank or promotion would in any way be affected by its proceedings; and two members, at least, if practicable, shall be of equal rank with the officer to be examined. The officers constituting such board shall receive the same pay and allowances for traveling expenses as members of courts-martial.

Officers whose commissions § 92. No officer, whose commission shall have been vacated under the next preceding section, shall be eligible for election to any military office for the period of one year, and his election shall be void; and in case the vacancy so created shall not within thirty days be filled by the election of some other and proper person, the commander-in-chief shall have power to fill such vacancy by appointment. *have been vacated.*

§ 93. If any commissioned officer shall have become or shall hereafter become incapable of performing the duties of his office, he shall be placed upon the supernumerary list, and withdrawn from active service and command. *Incapacity.*

§ 94. In order to carry out the provisions of this act, the commander-in-chief shall from time to time, as occasion may require, cause to assemble a board of not less than three nor more than five commissioned officers, one of whom at least shall be of the medical staff, to determine the facts as to the nature and occasion of the disability of such officers as appear disabled or unfit from any cause to perform military service, such board being hereby invested with the powers of a court of inquiry and court-martial, and their decision shall be subject to like revision as that of such courts by the commander-in-chief. The board whenever it finds an officer incapacitated for active service, shall report such fact to the commander-in-chief, and if he approve such judgment, the disabled officer shall thereupon be placed upon the supernumerary list according to the provisions of this act; provided always, that the members of the board shall in every case be sworn to an honest and impartial performance of their duties, and that no officer shall be placed upon the supernumerary list by the action of said board, without having had a fair and full hearing before the board, if upon due summons he shall demand it, nor shall any officer be summoned before such board unless reported to the commander-in-chief as incapable by a majority of the commissioned officers of his regiment, brigade or division, as the case may be. *Retiring board.*

§ 95. In time of war, insurrection, invasion, or imminent danger thereof, when the military forces of this state shall be in the actual service thereof, the commander-in-chief shall have power, whenever the public interests may in his opinion so require to suspend from active service such officer or officers as he shall deem it discreet, so to suspend and fill the vacancy thus created by appointment; but no *Suspension.*

THE MILITIA LAW

such suspension shall continue for a longer period than thirty days, unless a court-martial shall have in the meantime been ordered for the trial of such officer or officers.

OF THE ORGANIZATION OF THE STAFF DEPARTMENTS.

Aids of commander-in-chief.
§ 96. The commander-in-chief shall be entitled to three aids, with the rank of colonel; and a military secretary, with the rank of major.

Aids of major-generals and brigadiers.
§ 97. Each major-general shall be entitled to two aids, with the rank of major; and each brigadier-general to one aid, with the rank of captain.

Adjutant-general, assistant adjutant-general, inspectors.
§ 98. The adjutant-general shall have the rank of brigadier-general; and in his department there shall be an assistant adjutant-general, with the rank of colonel; to each division a division inspector, with the rank of colonel; to each brigade a brigade inspector, to serve also as a brigade major, with the rank of major; and to each regiment or battalion, an adjutant, with the rank of lieutenant.

Inspector-general, rank and duties. Assistant inspector-general.
§ 99. The inspector-general shall have the rank of brigadier-general, and his duty shall be to attend to the organization of the militia of this state. He shall inspect every branch connected with the military service, attend the military parades and encampments, when other official duties will permit, and report annually to the commander-in-chief. In the inspector-general's department, there shall be an assistant inspector-general, with the rank of colonel, who shall also act under the direction of the inspector-general, as inspector of military accounts.

Engineer-in-chief, division, brigade and regimental engineers.
§ 100. The engineer-in-chief shall have the rank of brigadier-general; and there shall be in his department to each division, a division engineer, with the rank of colonel; to each brigade, a brigade engineer, with the rank of major; to each regiment, one engineer, with the rank of captain.

Quartermaster-general, his rank, brigade and regimental quartermasters. Storekeepers.
§ 101. In the quartermaster-general's department there shall be a quartermaster-general, with the rank of brigadier-general; to each division, a division quartermaster, with the rank of lieutenant-colonel; to each brigade, a brigade quartermaster, with the rank of captain; and to each regiment or battalion, a quartermaster, with the rank of lieutenant; and the quartermaster-general may, with the approval of the commander-in-chief, appoint so many store-

keepers as the exigencies of the service may require, not exceeding one to each storehouse.

§ 102. In the department of the commissary-general of subsistence, there shall be a commissary-general of subsistence, with the rank of colonel; and in his department there shall be so many assistant commissaries, with the rank of captain, as the exigencies of the service may require; such assistant commissaries to be appointed by the commander-in-chief, and to hold their offices during his pleasure. Commissary-general of subsistence. Assistant commissaries.

§ 103. In the paymaster-general's department there shall be a paymaster-general, with the rank of colonel; to each division, a division paymaster, with the rank of major; and to each brigade, a brigade paymaster, with the rank of captain; but such paymasters may at any time be detached from the service in said brigades or divisions. Paymaster-general, division and brigade paymasters.

§ 104. The commissary-general shall hereafter be known as the commissary-general of ordnance, and shall have the rank of brigadier-general; and in his department there shall be an assistant, with the rank of colonel; and so many military storekeepers, for the safe keeping and the preservation of the state arsenals, magazines, fortifications and military stores belonging to this state, as he may find it necessary to appoint, not exceeding one to each arsenal. Commissary-general of ordnance, assistant commissary, military storekeepers.

§ 105. In the hospital department there shall be a surgeon-general, with the rank of brigadier-general; to each division, a hospital surgeon, with the rank of colonel; to each brigade, a hospital surgeon, with the rank of major; to each regiment, a surgeon, with the rank of captain; and to each regiment or battalion, a surgeon's mate, with the rank of lieutenant; but such rank shall not entitle said officers to promotions in the line, nor regulate their pay or rations in the service; and all such officers shall be graduates of an incorporated school or college of medicine. Surgeon-general, division, brigade and regimental surgeons and surgeons mates.

§ 106. To each regiment or battalion there shall be appointed one chaplain, who shall be a regular ordained minister of a Christian denomination. Chaplains.

§ 107. In the judge-advocate's department there shall be a judge-advocate-general, with the rank of brigadier-general; to each division, a division judge-advocate, with the rank of colonel; and to each brigade, brigade judge-advocate, with the rank of major. Judge-advocate-general, division and brigade judge-advocates.

§ 108. There shall be to each regiment or battalion two sergeant standard-bearers, one sergeant-major, one quartermaster sergeant, one commissary sergeant, and one drum major; and to each regiment or battalion of light artillery and cavalry, one trumpet major.

<small>Sergeant standard bearers, sergeant-majors, drum-majors, commissary-sergeants, trumpet-majors.</small>

§ 109. The chief of each staff department shall, under the direction of the commander-in-chief, have command over all subordinate officers in his department, and shall, from time to time, issue orders and instructions for their government and practice.

<small>Staff departments, powers of chiefs of.</small>

§ 110. The commander-in-chief is hereby authorized and empowered to organize, in his discretion, the various staff departments, and to prescribe by rules and regulations the duties to be performed by the officers connected therewith, which shall, as far as may be, conform to those which are prescribed for the government of the staff department in the army of the United States.

<small>Staff departments to be organized by commander-in-chief.</small>

§ 111. Each chief of such department shall prepare and transmit, at the expense of this state, all blank forms of returns, precepts, warrants and proceedings necessary in his department.

<small>Blanks, warrants, &c.</small>

OF THE ORGANIZATION OF BANDS OF MUSICIANS.

§ 112. The commanding officer of each regiment or battalion may, in his discretion, organize a band of musicians, and by warrant, under his hand, may appoint a leader of such band.

<small>Bands, how organized. Leader, how appointed.</small>

§ 113. Such musicians shall be subject to the orders of such leader, and be under the command of the commanding officer of the regiment or battalion; and the whole or any part of said band may be required by such commanding officer to appear at any meeting of the officers for military purposes, and at the review and inspection or encampment of such regiment or battalion.

<small>Musicians, duties of.</small>

§ 114. The leader of each band shall, whenever required by such commanding officer, make returns to him of the warning of the members of his band, and of the delinquencies therein, which returns shall be duly authenticated by the oath of such leader, taken before a field officer of such regiment or battalion.

<small>Duties of leader of band.</small>

§ 115. Such return, so sworn to, shall be received as evidence in all cases, in the same manner as like returns of non-commissioned officers of infantry companies. *Return of delinquent musicians.*

§ 116. Such commanding officer shall make the like returns of all such delinquents and delinquencies, as in cases of non-commissioned officers and musicians in companies of infantry, and with like effect, and the courts-martial shall impose the like penalties on such delinquent members of said band. *Penalties.*

§ 117. The commanding officer of such regiment or battalion shall have authority to disband such band, whether now or hereafter established, and to revoke the warrant of its leader. *Band may be disbanded.*

§ 118. The provisions of this article shall apply to all musicians employed to serve with the military forces of this state. *General provisions.*

OF THE ISSUING AND SAFE KEEPING OF ARMS.

§ 119. Whenever any company, organized under the provisions of this act, shall have reached the minimum number of thirty-two non-commissioned officers and privates, the supervisors of the county in which such company district is situated shall, upon the demand of the captain or commandant of such company, countersigned by the colonel of the regiment, together with the certificate of the adjutant-general, that such company comprises thirty-two non-commissioned officers and privates, erect or rent within the bounds of such regiment, for said company, a suitable and convenient armory, drill room, and place of deposit for the safe keeping of such arms, uniforms, equipments, accoutrements and camp equipage, as shall be furnished such company under the provisions of this act, except in such places where a public armory shall then exist, the same armory to be used by several companies, or a regimental or battalion armory to be used by all the companies, as the inspector-general shall deem expedient. *Armories, when furnished.*

§ 120. The expense of erecting or renting such armories shall be a portion of the county charges of such county, and shall be levied and raised in the same manner as other county charges are levied and paid. *Expense a county charge.*

§ 121. In case such armory shall not be erected or rented by the supervisors for the use of such company, the com- *Armories, how provided if su-*

mandant of the regiment, in his discretion, with the approval of the inspector-general, may rent a room or building to be used for the purpose of such armory, and the amount of rent thereof, provided the same shall not exceed the sum of two hundred and fifty dollars for each company, in the several cities of this state, and fifty dollars for companies not located in cities, shall be a county charge, and shall be paid by such supervisors, and levied and raised as hereinbefore provided.

Armory under direction of commandant of regiment.

§ 122. Such armory, when erected or rented, shall be under the control and charge of the commanding officer of the regiment in whose bounds or district it shall be located; and such commanding officer shall deposit therein all arms and equipments received from time to time for the use of any company in his regiment.

Commissary-general to furnish arms.

§ 123. The commissary-general of the state shall furnish, on the order of the commander-in-chief, all necessary arms and equipments, suited to the particular company or corps belonging to each regiment, required for camp and field duty; the same to be furnished at the expense of the state, including transportation. But no arms or equipments shall be furnished to any company or corps, unless such company or corps shall be connected with the regular military organization of the state.

Commandants of regiments to be responsible for safe keeping of arms.

§ 124. The commanding officer of each regiment or company shall be responsible for the safe keeping and return of all arms and equipments committed to his charge, and shall execute such bonds as the commander-in-chief shall require from time to time; and no company shall be so furnished until bonds for the safe keeping and return shall be made out and approved by the commander-in-chief, and until a suitable armory or place of deposit shall be assigned, rented or erected, in such regiment.

Arms, how distributed.

§ 125. The commanding officer of any regiment or company who shall have received, according to the provisions of this act, any arms and equipments from the state for the use of his regiment or company, shall distribute the same to his regiment or company, as he shall deem proper, and require of those to whom they were distributed to return them at such time and place as he shall order and direct; and any officer who shall neglect or refuse to comply with such order, shall forfeit the sum not to exceed double the price of any arms or equipments he shall have received, to be sued for and collected in the name of the commandant of the regiment for the use of the military fund of such regiment.

§ 126. The commanding officer of each regiment shall appoint a suitable person to take charge of the armory, armories or place of deposit of his regiment, or of the several companies in his regiment, and all arms, equipments, and other property of the state therein deposited, and to discharge all duties connected therewith, as shall be from time to time prescribed by the commanding officer. Armorer, how appointed.

§ 127. Such person so appointed shall receive a compensation not to exceed one dollar per day for the time actually employed in cleaning guns, and other duties indispensably necessary for the safe keeping and preservation of such property of the state as shall be committed to his charge. Compensation.

§ 128. The commander-in-chief shall, from time to time, make such orders, rules and regulations as he may deem proper for the observance of all officers having charge of any armory in which arms of the people of this state shall be deposited. Armories rules for their government.

§ 129. Whenever the commissioned officers of any uniformed company in this state shall make application to the commanding officer of their regiment for any arms or equipments suited to the corps to which their company may belong, and who shall, at the same time, furnish such commanding officer with sufficient bonds for the safe keeping and return of the same, he may deliver to such officers such arms and equipments belonging to this state as he shall deem proper; but no such arms or equipments shall be delivered, unless the bonds given for the safe keeping and return thereof shall be approved by the sureties who became responsible in the bonds furnished to the commander-in-chief for all such arms and equipments. Arms, how distributed to companies.

§ 130. Any person who shall willfully injure such armory, or its fixtures, or any gun, sword, pistol or other property of the state therein deposited, shall be deemed guilty of a misdemeanor. Penalty for injuring arms.

§ 131. The commissary-general may, from time to time, require any officer to examine any armory provided as Arms, &c., to be examined.

aforesaid, and report to him the condition thereof, and of the arms and camp equipage therein deposited.

Camp equipage, how furnished and returned.

§ 132. All officers applying for the issue of camp equipage shall set forth in their application the number of tents which they will require, the time when their respective regiments or companies go into camp, and the number of days which such encampment will continue; and the commanding officer of each camp shall, immediately after the breaking up of the encampment, cause the equipage to be returned to such of the state arsenals, or turned over to such officer as may be directed by the adjutant-general; provided, however, that such tents and camp equipage shall be deposited in some one of the state arsenals on or before the first day of November in each year.

OF THE DRILLS, PARADES, AND RENDEZVOUS OF THE NATIONAL GUARD, AND OF COMPENSATION FOR MILITARY SERVICES.

Annual inspection.

§ 133. Whenever any company or companies shall be organized, uniformed and equipped in any regimental district of this state, such company or companies shall parade annually thereafter by regiment, battalion or company, at such time and place, between the first day of May and the first day of November, as the commanding officers of their respective brigades shall order and direct, for the purpose of discipline, inspection and review. At any such parade, all the commissioned and non-commissioned officers, musicians and privates shall appear and discharge any and all the duties required to be performed by the commanding officer. No person shall be permitted in the ranks on any parade who does not appear in full uniform, and armed and equipped suited to the company to which he belongs; and no person shall be permitted in the ranks who is not fully armed and equipped according to the provisions of this act and the laws of the United States; and all members who shall appear without such arms and equipments, or without a uniform at any parade, shall be returned as absent from parade, and fined accordingly.

Parade and drills, number of, how ordered.

§ 134. In addition to the annual inspection herein specified, there shall be six drills or parades of the national guard in each year, not less than three of which shall be by regiment or battalion, and at such times and places as the commander-in-chief, commandant of division, brigade, regiment or battalion, shall direct.

§ 135. The commanding officer, at any parade, may cause those under his command to perform any field or camp duty he shall require; and also to put under guard for the day or time of continuing such parade, any officer, musician or private, who shall disobey the orders of his superior officer, or in any way interrupt the exercises of the day; also, all other persons who shall trespass on the parade ground, or in any way or manner interrupt or molest the orderly discharge of duty of those under arms; and also may prohibit and prevent the sale of all spirituous liquors within one mile of such parade or encampment; and also, in his discretion, all hucksters or auction sales, or gambling may be abated as nuisances. *Powers of commanding officer at parades.*

§ 136. In addition to the drills and parades above specified, the commanding officers of companies may require the officers, non-commissioned officers, musicians and privates of their companies to meet for company drill and parade once in each month, from November to May, and so much oftener as a majority of the members of such company shall prescribe in and by the by-laws for the government of the same. *Company drills.*

§ 137. No parade or rendezvous of the national guard shall be ordered on any day during which a general or special election shall be held, nor within five days previous to such election, except in cases of riot, invasion or insurrection or of imminent danger thereof; and if any officer shall order any such parade or rendezvous, he shall forfeit and pay to the people of this state the sum of five hundred dollars. *Parades not to be held within 5 days previous to election.*

§ 138. For the purpose of warning the non-commissioned officers, musicians and privates to any parade, encampment, or place of rendezvous, the commandant of each company shall issue his orders, under his hand, to his non-commissioned officers, or to such of them as he may deem proper, requiring them respectively to warn all the non-commissioned officers, musicians and privates of his company to appear at such parade, encampment, or place of rendezvous, armed and equipped, according to law and regulation. *Warnings to attend parade, how served.*

Service.	§ 139. Each non-commissioned officer, to whom such order shall be directed, shall warn every person whom he shall be therein required to warn, by reading the orders, or stating the substance thereof in the hearing of such person; or in case of his absence, by leaving a notice thereof at his usual place of abode or business, with some person of suitable age and discretion, or by sending the same to him by mail, directed to him at the post office nearest his place of residence.
Returns of warnings, how made.	§ 140. Such non-commissioned officer shall make a return to his commandant, in which he shall state the names of all persons by him warned, and the manner of warning them respectively, and shall make oath to the truth of such return, which oath shall be administered by the commandant, and certified by him on the warrant or return.
To whom delivered.	§ 141. Such commandant shall deliver the return, together with his own return of all delinquencies, to the president of the proper court-martial.
Return to be evidence.	§ 142. The return of such non-commissioned officer, so sworn to and certified, shall be as good evidence, on the trial of any person returned as a delinquent, of the facts therein stated, as if such officer had testified to the same before the court-martial on such trial.
Return of delinquencies of non-commissioned officers, how made.	§ 143. Every commandant of a company shall make the like return, upon honor, and with like effect, of every delinquency and neglect of duty of his non-commissioned officers, either in not attending on any parade or encampment, or not executing or returning a warrant to them directed, or not obeying the orders of their commanding officers; and also the names of every non-commissioned officer, musician or private who shall refuse or neglect to obey the orders of his superior officer, or to perform such military duty or exercise as may be required, or depart from his colors, post or guard, or leave the ranks without permission from his superior officer.
Commissioned officer may warn without warrant.	§ 144. Any commissioned officer of a company may, without a warrant, warn any or all of the members of his company to appear at any parade, encampment or place of rendezvous. Such warning may be given by him, either personally or by leaving or affixing a notice in the same manner as if given by a non-commissioned officer; and his

certificate, upon honor, shall be received by any court-martial as legal evidence of such warning.

§ 145. Nothing in the provisions of this act shall be so construed as to preclude, in the absence of a proper return, the giving in evidence, at any court-martial upon trial for delinquencies, neglects of duty or offense whatsoever, matters of facts which go to substantiate the charge or offense; but all such proof shall be received under the usual rule of evidence in courts of justice.

Evidence of delinquencies in absence of return.

§ 146. Every non-commissioned officer, musician and private, of any uniform corps of this state, shall be holden to duty therein for the term of seven years from his enlistment, unless disability after enlistment shall incapacitate him to perform such duty, or he shall be regularly discharged by the commandant of his regiment; all general and staff officers; all field officers, and all commissioned and non-commissioned officers, musicians and privates, of the military forces of this state, shall be exempt from jury duty during the time they shall perform military duty, and from the payment of highway taxes, not exceeding six days in any one year; and every such person not assessed for highway taxes shall be entitled to a deduction, in the assessment of his real and personal property, to the amount of five hundred dollars; and every person who shall have served seven years, and shall have been honorably discharged, as required by this section, shall forever after, so long as he remains a citizen of this state, be exempt from two days' highway taxes in each year; and if a resident of any city of this state, he shall forever be entitled to a deduction in the assessment of his real and personal property, to the amount of five hundred dollars each year; the exemption and deduction herein provided for to be allowed only on the production, to the assessor or assessors of the town or ward in which he resides, of a certificate from the commanding officer of the regiment in which he last served.

Term of service.

Exemptions from jury duty, highway taxes, &c.

§ 147. All notices, warrants or summons for officers, non-commissioned officers, musicians and privates of any company or troop, to attend a drill, improvement meeting or court-martial, may be served either personally or by leaving a written or printed notice, containing the substance of such notice, warrant or summons, at the dwelling-house, store, counting-house or usual place of business of the

Service of warrants, notices, &c.

person to be notified, warned or summoned, with some person of suitable age and discretion; and any officer, non-commissioned officer, musician or private, may also be warned to attend any parade, encampment or drill, by enclosing a notice, directed to him at his place of residence, by mail, directed to him at his nearest post-office, at least five days before the service required of him.

Service of notices upon officers.

§ 148. The officers and non-commissioned staff officers of each regiment shall be warned to attend any parade or drill in the same manner as is prescribed by law for the warning of the privates of any company, and the commanding officer of each regiment may designate and order any or all of the non-commissioned staff officers of the regiment to perform that duty, who shall make return thereof to the commanding officer, or the adjutant of the regiment, in the same manner, and under the same penalties for delinquencies, as are by law imposed on non-commissioned officers of companies for similar delinquencies.

Orders for encampments and parades, how published.

§ 149. All orders for encampment, inspection and review shall be published at least twenty days previous to such parade, in such manner as the commandant of the brigade shall direct, and notice thereof shall at the same time be given to the inspector-general; and all commanding officers of regiments, battalions or companies, may, on any parade, read brigade, regimental or battalion orders, and notify their several commands to appear as specified in said brigade or regimental order for the purposes therein contained, which notice shall be sufficient warning to all persons present.

Non-attendance, how punished.

§ 150. Every officer, non-commissioned officer, musician and private of any uniformed company, who shall unnecessarily neglect to appear on the days at the time and place appointed for such duty, agreeably to the provisions of this act, shall be subject to such fines and penalties as are hereinafter provided.

Drills of officers and non-commissioned officers.

§ 151. The commanding officer of any brigade, regiment or battalion, in addition to the rendezvous above prescribed, may require the commissioned officers and non-commissioned officers to meet for exercise and improvement, at such times and places as he shall appoint; and he may require them to appear with such arms and accoutrements as he may prescribe; said officers shall thereupon be formed into a corps of instruction, without regard to rank, and shall be thoroughly instructed in the manual of arms, the school of the soldier and company, and in such other theoretical and practical details of duty as the said commanding officer shall deem proper.

§ 152. Each commandant of division may review either one of the brigades in his division in each year; and he shall require the officers of the division staff, armed and equipped as the law and regulations direct, to accompany him. *Major-general to review brigades.*

§ 153. The commandant of each brigade shall attend, with the officers of the brigade staff, armed and equipped as the law and regulation direct, the annual inspection and review of the several regiments and battalions in his brigade. *Brigadier-general to attend inspection.*

§ 154. It shall be the duty of commandants of companies, at the annual inspection, to furnish the brigade inspector with a return which shall show: *Duties of commandants of companies at annual inspection.*

1. The number of commissioned, non-commissioned officers, musicians and privates of his company or troop present on parade, designating the number of each.

2. The number of such company absent from parade.

3. The uniforms, arms and equipments inspected.

4. The number of uniforms belonging to said company or troop.

5. The arms and equipments in the possession of said company or troop.

§ 155. It shall be the duty of each commandant of a regiment or battalion, within twenty days after the annual inspection, to furnish the brigade inspector with a return of the field and staff officers, non-commissioned staff officers, musicians of said regiment or battalion, present and absent, armed and equipped and uniformed according to law and regulation. *Duties of commandants of regiments as to annual inspection.*

§ 156. At all encampments, the brigade inspector shall attend on the first day thereof, to superintend the exercises and manœuvres, and to introduce the system of discipline which is or shall be prescribed by law; and on such day he shall take the command as drill officer, so far as shall be necessary to the execution of those duties; and he shall also make an annual inspection at such times as the commanding officer of the brigade shall order and direct. *Brigade inspector to attend encampments.*

THE MILITIA LAW

Brigade inspectors to report to adjutant-general.

§ 157. It shall be the duty of the brigade inspector to transmit a copy of the inspection return, annually, to the adjutant-general, and a duplicate of the same to the division inspector, within thirty days after the inspection shall be made.

Brigade inspectors to transmit statement to adjutant-general.

§ 158. It shall be the duty of the brigade inspector, within thirty days after the annual review in each year, to transmit to the adjutant-general a statement of the reviews and inspection of the several regiments or battalions in his brigade, attended by the commanding officer of division, accompanied by division staff, armed and equipped and uniformed according to law and regulation, and also the commanding officer of brigade, with the brigade staff, armed and equipped according to law and regulation.

General officer's absence of from inspection.

§ 159. In case any general officer or any member of his staff shall neglect to attend such inspection and review, it shall be the duty of the adjutant-general to require such officer to render an excuse in writing to the commander-in-chief for his delinquency. If the commander-in-chief shall deem such excuse insufficient, he shall order a court-martial to try the delinquency.

Uniform companies may form by-laws.

§ 160. Each uniform company may form by-laws, rules and regulations, not inconsistent with this act for the government and improvement of its members in military science; and when approved of by two-thirds of all the members belonging to any such company, shall be binding; but may be altered from time to time as may become necessary.

Penalty for violation of company by-laws.

§ 161. For violations of the by-laws of any uniformed company, the non-commissioned officer, musician or private offending, by a vote of the company, three-fifths being present, may be expelled from the company; and upon the action of the company being confirmed in orders by the commandant of the regiment, the name of such person or persons shall be stricken from the roll of such company, his certificate of membership shall be surrendered and canceled, and he or they shall cease to be a member or members of such company; and his or their term of service in said company shall not be allowed under the provisions of this act.

Adjutant-general to prescribe

§ 162. The adjutant-general shall prescribe the form of enlisting orders to be furnished and used by each company or troop in recruiting or filling up such company or troop with its required number. form of enlisting orders.

§ 163. The commandants of division shall discharge the duties, possess the powers, and be liable to the penalties pertaining to their office, as granted by law or military custom, provided that no division parades, except of the first division, or in case of invasion, insurrection, or to aid the civil authorities, shall be ordered without the consent of the commander-in-chief. Major-general powers and duties.

§ 164. The commander-in-chief may order such parades or drills of the uniformed troops, or any part of them, as he shall deem proper. Commander-in-chief may order parades and drills.

§ 165. There shall be a camp of instruction once in each year after the present year, in each of the division districts of this state, if the commander-in-chief shall so order, to be held at such time and in such manner as he shall direct; and the commander-in-chief is hereby authorized and empowered to order such companies and regiments from such division districts, respectively, to attend such camps as he may deem proper, but in such manner that all the companies and regiments therein shall be ordered to attend such camp from year to year in rotation, provided, always, that not more than ten thousand men in any one year shall be ordered to attend said camps; and in case suitable ground cannot be found in any district for said camp, the same may be held in the adjoining district. Camp of instruction.

§ 166. Such camps shall continue for a period not exceeding ten days, and shall be governed by the rules and regulations of the army of the United States. Duration and government of camps.

§ 167. The commander-in-chief is hereby authorized and empowered, at his discretion, to order such regiments, battalions, batteries, or companies as he shall deem proper, and without regard to arm, not, however, exceeding one thousand men in any one year, to be stationed at such forts or other places as may be furnished by the United States government, or as may be convenient for that purpose within the State of New York for a period not exceeding ten days in any one year, for instruction in the management of heavy artillery for sea and lake coast defense under such instructors as he shall assign for that purpose. Lake and sea-coast defense.

§ 168. The commander-in-chief shall designate commissioned officers of proper rank, without regard to military Commandants and instructors districts, to command such camps, forts or other places, and shall assign such other officers, also without regard to military districts, to duty as field and staff officers and instructors, as may be required to fully officer such camps and forts.

Commissary-general to furnish ordnance and ammunition.

§ 169. The commissary-general of ordnance shall furnish, upon the requisition of the commander-in-chief, such arms, ordnance and ammunition as may be necessary for the use of the military forces so encamped or stationed.

Quartermaster-general to furnish tents and camp equipage.

§ 170. The quartermaster-general shall, upon the requisition of the commander-in-chief, furnish such tents, camp equipage, or other state property as may be required for the use of the military forces so encamped or stationed, and shall also furnish the transportation necessary for conveying said forces to and from such camps or stations.

Commissary-general of subsistence to furnish subsistence

§ 171. The commissary-general of subsistence shall, upon the requisition of the commander-in-chief, provide the subsistence necessary for said forces, such subsistence to conform in price and quantity to the ration prescribed by the general regulations for the army of the United States, and to be issued in kind.

Commander-in-chief to draw his warrant on treasury.

§ 172. The commander-in-chief is hereby authorized and empowered to draw his warrant upon the state treasury for such sum as shall be required by the engineer and quartermaster of said camps, forts or stations, in laying out and preparing the ground designated for such purpose, and in furnishing quarters for said forces and for the services of the officers, instructors and privates ordered to attend the same; also for all necessary expenses of said forces, including transportation and subsistence; such expenses to be audited by a board to consist of the commander-in-chief, comptroller, state treasurer and inspector-general.

OF COMPENSATION FOR MILITARY SERVICES.

Pay in time of war.

§ 173. The military forces of this state, when in the actual service of the state in time of war, insurrection, invasion or imminent danger thereof, shall, during their time of service, be entitled to the same pay, rations and allowances for clothing as are or may hereafter be established by law for the army of the United States.

Pay at encampments, &c.

§ 174. There shall be paid to such officers, non-commissioned officers and privates as shall be specially ordered to attend encampments, and sea and lake coast defense duty, in pursuance of the provisions of this act, not to exceed the following sum each, for every day actually on duty:

1. To all non-commissioned officers, musicians and privates, one dollar.

2. To all commissioned officers of the line below the rank of captain, two dollars.

3. To all commanding officers of companies, three dollars.

4. To all field officers below the rank of colonel, four dollars.

5. To all commanding officers of regiments, five dollars.

6. To all regimental staff officers, two dollars and fifty cents, and to all non-commissioned staff officers, one dollar and fifty cents.

7. To all brigadier-generals, six dollars.

8. To all brigade staff officers, four dollars.

9. To all major-generals, eight dollars.

10. To all division staff officers, five dollars.

11. All mounted officers, and all members of any company of cavalry or artillery, mounted or equipped, shall receive one dollar per day for each horse actually used by them.

12. To each military storekeeper, such sum, not exceeding twenty-five dollars per annum, as the commander-in-chief shall think proper to allow.

§ 175. The staff of the commander-in-chief, and the assistants in the several departments, in lieu of all compensation and allowances now provided by law in time of peace, when upon actual duty under the provisions of this act, either at drills, parades, encampments, lake and sea coast defense duty, or otherwise, shall receive such compensation as is provided in this act for officers of the same rank, with their necessary and proper expenses, and those of their departments, to be paid by the state, upon the certificate of the commander-in-chief. *Pay of staff of commander-in-chief in time of peace.*

§ 176. In case of war, insurrection, rebellion or invasion, or imminent danger thereof, when the military forces of the State of New York, or any part thereof, shall be in the actual service of the state, or in the service of the United States, the staff of the commander-in-chief, while on duty, the assistants and clerks in the several staff departments, *Pay of staff of commander-in-chief in time of war.*

and such other officers as may be detailed by the commander-in-chief for the performance of any duties connected with the recruiting, mustering, enrolling, equipping, arming, providing and administering of justice for such forces, shall, in lieu of all other allowances under this act, receive such reasonable and proper compensation, not exceeding the pay and allowances of officers of the same rank in the service of the United States, as the commander-in-chief shall deem proper, together with their necessary expenses, and those of their departments, to be paid by the state upon the certificate of the commander-in-chief, showing a detailed statement of such services and expenses.

Pay of clerks in staff departments.

§ 177. Such clerks shall be employed in the several departments of the general staff of this state as shall be actually necessary for the public service, in the opinion of the commander-in-chief, and they shall receive, for the time they may be actually necessarily employed, such compensation as the commander-in-chief shall prescribe, not exceeding, however, in any case, the rate of twelve hundred dollars per annum.

Pay-roll of non-commissioned officers and privates.

§ 178. The commanding officer of every uniformed company which shall have been ordered into camp, or to perform sea and lake coast defense duty, in accordance with the provisions of this act, shall, at the close of the term for which such company shall have been ordered to such camp or duty, make out an alphabetical list of the members of his company who shall have appeared and performed such duty, uniformed, armed and equipped, as the law and regulations direct, and shall set opposite to each name the number of days each shall have performed duty, and the amount of pay each is entitled to receive for such service and deliver the same, certified on oath to be correct and true, to the commanding officer of the camp or post, who shall immediately cause the same to be transcribed in a book or books to be kept by him for that purpose; such company commandant shall also set forth, opposite to the name of each member of his company, whether such member is indebted to the state in any and what amount on account of his uniform and equipments.

Pay-roll of officers.

§ 179. The commanding officer of the camp or post shall, also, at the close of the time for which each company, battery, battalion or regiment shall have been ordered to

OF THE STATE OF NEW YORK. 41

attend for duty thereat, make or cause to be made a complete roster or list of all commissioned officers and non-commissioned staff officers who shall have appeared and performed duty at such parade or encampment, uniformed, armed and equipped, as the law and regulations direct, and shall set opposite to each name the number of days each shall have performed duty at such encampment or post, and the amount of pay each is entitled to receive for such service, and shall immediately cause the said list to be transcribed in a book or books to be kept by him for that purpose.

§ 180. The commander-in-chief shall draw his warrant upon the comptroller for the amount which shall become due to officers, non-commissioned officers and privates, for services rendered at the drills and encampments for which payment is allowed by this act. *Commander-in-chief to draw warrant for pay due under this act.*

§ 181. The paymaster-general, or a division or brigade paymaster under his directions, shall, once in each year, visit the different regimental districts of this state, and shall pay to the officers, non-commissioned officers and privates, such sums as they may be entitled to receive therefor under this act. *Paymaster-general or other paymasters to pay such amounts as may be due for services.*

§ 182. The commander-in-chief shall have power to prescribe such further rules and regulations to provide for the more convenient payment of all sums which may become due to officers, non-commissioned officers and privates, under the provisions of this act; and the paymaster-general, under the direction of the commander-in-chief, shall prepare the necessary forms and pay rolls, and cause the same to be transmitted to the commandants of such regiments, camps and posts. *Rules as to pay to be prescribed by commander-in-chief.*

OF THE REGIMENTAL FUND AND REGIMENTAL BOARDS OF AUDITORS.

§ 183. The comptroller shall annually draw his warrant upon the treasurer in favor of the county treasurer of each county, for the sum of five hundred dollars for each regiment or battalion, certified by the adjutant-general, to be organized according to the provisions of this act, within his county, which sum, together with the fines collected from delinquent officers, non-commissioned officers, musi- *$500 to be paid to each regiment as regimental fund.*

cians and privates, shall constitute the military fund of such regiment.

<small>Regimental board of auditors.</small>
§ 184. There shall be a board of officers in each regiment which shall consist of the commanding officer of the brigade, who shall be president thereof, and of the field officers of the regiment and the senior captain therein, any three of whom shall form a quorum for business, the commanding officer of the brigade being one.

<small>Brigadier-general to convene board of auditors.</small>
§ 185. The commandant of each brigade shall, from time to time, as he shall deem necessary, convene the board of officers of each regiment created by this act.

<small>Powers and duties of regimental boards.</small>
§ 186. Such board, when so convened, shall audit all just claims on the military fund of such regiment for contingent expenses of the regiment, and shall make their order on the proper county treasurer, which shall require him to pay such order out of any money in his hands belonging to the military fund of such regiment.

<small>Regimental board to enter proceeding in a book.</small>
<small>Pay of members.</small>
§ 187. Such board may also direct such printing and publishing to be performed and executed as shall be necessary for the best interest of the regiment and service; the members of such board shall be entitled to receive for each day's service, as such members, the sum of two dollars, for not more than three days in any one year, such sum to be certified and paid in the same manner. Such board shall enter their proceedings, from time to time, in a book to be kept for that purpose by each regiment.

<small>County treasurers to report amount of funds in their hands.</small>
§ 188. All county and city treasurers shall report to the brigadier-general, within the bounds of whose brigades he may reside, the amount of all moneys received by them, respectively, by the first days of April and December, annually, and the balance then remaining in their hands, and the number of the regiment to which the same belongs.

OF THE COURTS OF INQUIRY AND COURTS-MARTIAL.

Of the Courts of Inquiry and Courts-Martial for the Trial of Officers.

<small>Court of Inquiry.</small>
§ 189. Courts of inquiry may be instituted by the commander-in-chief, or the commanding officer of division or brigade, in relation to those officers for whose trial they are authorized to appoint courts-martial, for the purpose of investigating the conduct of any officer, either by his own

OF THE STATE OF NEW YORK. 43

solicitation, or on a complaint or charge of improper conduct, degrading to the character of an officer, or for the purpose of settling rank; but no such court shall consist of more than one officer, who may, if approved of by the officer ordering the court, require a judge-advocate to attend such court in taking testimony, and in investigating any complaint that may come before such court.

§ 190. Such court shall, without delay, report the evidence adduced, a statement of facts, and an opinion thereon, when required to the officer instituting such court, who may in his discretion thereupon appoint a court-martial for the trial of the officer whose conduct shall have been inquired into. *Court of inquiry, duties, &c.*

§ 191. Every court-martial for the trial of a major-general shall be ordered by the commander-in-chief, and shall consist of five officers, any three of whom shall constitute a quorum. *Court-martial for trial of major-general, how ordered.*

§ 192. Every court-martial for the trial of a brigadier-general shall be ordered by the commander-in-chief, and shall consist of five officers, any three of whom shall constitute a quorum. *Court-martial for trial of brigadier-general.*

§ 193. All other courts-martial for the trial of commissioned officers shall consist of three officers, and shall be ordered, if for the trial of officers above rank of captain, by the commanding officer of division, and for all other officers, by the commanding officer of brigade. *Courts-martial, of whom to consist and how ordered.*

§ 194. No officer arrested shall be brought to trial, unless a copy of the charges and specifications, certified by the officer ordering the arrest, shall be delivered to him, or left at his usual place of abode, within three days after his arrest; nor unless the officer ordering such court-martial shall have ordered the same within thirty days after receiving notice of the arrest, and a copy of the charges and specifications; nor until ten days after a copy of a list of the names of the officers detailed to form the court shall have been delivered to the officer arrested, or left at his usual place of abode. *Charges and specifications and list of officers detailed to hold court to be served on accused.*

§ 195. The officer ordering the court may, at any time, supply any vacancy that, from any cause, may happen therein. *Vacancy may be supplied.*

§ 196. If the officer accused shall have any cause of challenge to any member of such court, he shall within a *Challenges.*

reasonable time after receiving a copy of the charges and a list of the members, deliver his cause of challenge, in writing, to the officer ordering such court, who shall thereupon determine as to the validity of such challenge; and if, in his opinion, the causes are sufficient, he shall appoint another member of such court.

Members of courts to be sworn.

§ 197. After the court shall be assembled, and after all challenges, if any are made, shall have been determined, the judge-advocate, whether commissioned or special, shall administer to each member the following oath:

"You,   , do swear that you will faithfully discharge the duties of a member of a court-martial now assembled, according to the best of your ability."

Judge-Advocate to keep proceedings secret.

§ 198. Every judge-advocate, whether commissioned or special, and every member of a court-martial, shall keep secret the sentence of the court, until the same shall be approved or disapproved according to law; and shall keep secret the vote or opinion of any particular member of the court, unless required to give evidence thereof by a court of justice.

Court-martial, sentence of.

§ 199. The sentence of any such court-martial shall be according to the nature and degree of the offense, and according to military usage, but shall not extend further, in time of peace, than cashiering the officer convicted, and disqualifying him from holding any office in the militia of this state, and imposing a fine not exceeding one hundred dollars.

Proceedings of court-martial to be delivered to officer ordering court.

§ 200. The proceedings and sentence of every court-martial shall, without delay, be delivered to the officer ordering the court, who shall approve or disapprove thereof, within fifteen days thereafter, and shall give notice of his approval or disapproval to the president of such court-martial and to the arresting officer, and he may, at his discretion, publish the sentence, as approved or disapproved, in orders; but no part of such sentence shall be executed until after the time allowed for appeal has expired.

Proceedings and sentence to be transmitted to adjutant-general's office.

§ 201. He also shall transmit such proceedings and sentence, and his approval or disapproval thereof, to the adjutant-general, to be kept in his office.

§ 202. The right of appeal to the commander-in-chief, as it now exists by military usage, is reserved; but no appeal shall be received, unless made within twenty days after the decision appealed from is made known to the person appealing. *Appeal to commander-in-chief.*

§ 203. There shall be allowed and paid out of the treasury, to each division and brigade judge-advocate, and to each president and member of any court of inquiry or court-martial for the trial of officers, two dollars for each day actually employed on duty; and the like compensation to every marshal appointed by any such court, for every day employed in the execution of the duties required of him. *Compensation of members of courts-martial.*

§ 204. The accounts of all persons who under this article are entitled to be paid out of the treasury, shall be audited by the comptroller, who shall, on the application of the governor, draw his warrant on the treasurer for such sums of money as may be requisite in the execution of the provisions of this act; and may require the chief of each staff department to account quarterly for all money received by him for the purposes connected with his department. *Accounts of all officers serving on courts-martial, how audited and paid.*

Of Regimental and Battalion Courts-Martial.

§ 205. The commandant of each brigade may at any time appoint a regimental or battalion court-martial for any regiment or battalion in his brigade, to consist, if practicable, of a field officer or captain. *Regimental courts-martial.*

§ 206. The appointment of said court shall be published in orders at least three weeks previous to the convening of the court; and the officer appointing said court shall fix the day on which it shall convene, and when convened, the court may adjourn from time to time as shall become necessary for the transaction of business, but the whole session of the court, from the day on which it shall convene until its dissolution, shall not exceed three weeks. *Appointment of regimental court-martial to be published.*

§ 207. In case any vacancy shall happen in the court, or a new court shall be required, the officer ordering the court, or his successor in command, may fill such vacancy or order a new court. *Vacancies, how filled.*

§ 208. The officer constituting such court, before he shall enter on his duties as such, shall take the following oath: *Oath.*

"I,   , do swear that I will well and truly try and determine, according to evidence, all matters between the people of the State of New York and any person or persons which shall come before the regimental (or battalion) court-martial to which I have been appointed."

Oath, how taken.

§ 209. Such oath shall be taken by the president, on or before the day on which the court shall convene, before a justice of the county in which he may reside, or a field officer of his regiment or battalion; and it shall be the duty of such justice or field officer to administer the oath without fee or reward.

Delinquents, how summoned.

§ 210. Such court shall direct a non-commissioned officer, or other fit person or persons, to be by him designated, to summon all delinquents and parties accused to appear before the court, at a time and place to be by him appointed, which service shall be personal, or by leaving such summons at the residence of such parties.

Returns of delinquents.

§ 211. Such non-commissioned officer, or other person or persons so designated, shall make the like return, and with like effect, as commissioned and non-commissioned officers are authorized and required to make, in cases of warning to a company or regimental parade, and shall be subject to the like penalties for neglect of duty.

Powers of regimental court-martial.

§ 212. The court, when organized, shall have the trial of all offenses, delinquencies and deficiencies, in the regiment or battalion for which it shall have been called, and shall have power to impose and direct to be levied all the fines to which non-commissioned officers, musicians or privates, are declared to be subject by the provisions of this act.

Appeal from decision.

§ 213. From the sentence of any such court, imposing a fine for any offense, delinquency or deficiency, an appeal, if made within twenty days, shall be allowed to the officer instituting the court, or to his successor in command, who may remit or mitigate such penalty or fine.

Compensation of members of regimental courts-martial.

§ 214. There shall be allowed and paid out of the military fund of said regiment:

1. To the officer constituting said court, a sum equal to one day's pay for field duty for each day he may be actually employed in holding the court or engaged in the business thereof, or in traveling to or from the court, allowing thirty miles for a day's travel.

2. To the non-commissioned officer or other person who shall have summoned delinquents to appear before the court, one dollar and twenty-five cents for each day he may have been necessarily so employed, and the same sum for each day of his attendance on the court. *Compensation of non-commissioned officer attending regimental courts-martial.*

3. Each officer to whom a warrant for the collection of fines may be directed, shall be entitled to the same fees, and be subject to the same penalties for any neglect, as are allowed and provided for on executions issued out of justices' courts.

4. For all other services and commitments under this act, the sheriff, jailer and constables executing the same, shall be entitled to the like fees as for similar services in other cases.

§ 215. All fines and penalties imposed by any regimental or battalion court-martial, shall be paid, by the officer collecting the same, to the treasurer of the county within which the officer instituting the court may reside, and shall belong to the military fund of such regiment. *Fines and penalties to be paid to county treasurer.*

OF THE IMPOSITION OF PENALTIES AND FINES FOR VIOLATING THE PROVISIONS OF THIS ACT.

§ 216. In time of peace, every commissioned officer, for disobedience of orders, neglect or ignorance of duty, unofficerlike conduct or disrespect to a superior officer, or for neglecting to furnish himself with a uniform and equipments within six months after receiving his commission, shall be arrested and brought to trial before a court-martial, who may, on conviction, sentence him to be cashiered, incapacitated from holding any military commission, or fined to an amount not exceeding one hundred dollars, or to be reprimanded, or may sentence him to all or either of such penalties, in their discretion. *Penalties for disobedience of orders, neglect of duty, &c.*

§ 217. Every commissioned officer refusing to pay over moneys in his hands, as is directed by the provisions of this act, shall be liable to be tried and cashiered, or otherwise punished therefor, by a court-martial. *Refusal to pay over moneys.*

§ 218. Every commissioned officer, and every non-commissioned officer, musician and private, shall, on due conviction, be subject for the following offenses, to the fines thereto annexed: *Penalties for sundry delinquencies.*

1. Every non-commissioned officer, musician and private, for non-appearance, when duly warned or summoned, at a company parade, a fine of two dollars; at a regimental or battalion parade or encampment, not less than three nor more than six dollars; and at a place of rendezvous, when called into actual service, a sum not exceeding twelve months' pay, nor less than one month's pay.

2. Every commissioned officer, for non-attendance at any parade or encampment, and every such officer, non-commissioned officer, musician and private, neglecting or refusing to obey the orders of his superior officers on any day of parade or encampment, or to perform such military duty or exercise as may be required, or departing from his colors, post or guard, or leaving his place or ranks without permission, a fine not more than one hundred nor less than five dollars.

3. For neglecting or refusing to obey any order or warrant to him lawfully given or directed, or to make a proper return thereof, if such return be necessary, or making a false return, or neglecting or refusing, when required, to summon a delinquent before a court-martial, or duly to return such summons, a fine not more than one hundred nor less than five dollars.

Officers refusing to act, how punished.
§ 219. Every commissioned officer, for neglecting or refusing to act as such when duly elected and commissioned, may be sentenced to pay a fine not less than ten dollars; every non-commissioned officer, for neglecting or refusing to act as such, when duly appointed and warranted, may be sentenced to pay a fine not less than five dollars; and every non-commissioned officer, for neglect of duty or disorderly or unofficerlike conduct, in addition to other penalties, may be reduced to the ranks by the commandant of the company, with the approbation of the commandant of the regiment or battalion.

Unlawful discharge of fire-arms.
§ 220. Every non-commissioned officer, musician or private, who shall unlawfully discharge any fire-arms within two miles of any parade, on the day thereof, shall be sentenced to pay a fine of one dollar.

Retaining commission, how punished.
§ 221. Any commissioned officer who shall retain a commission received by him for any subaltern for more than thirty days, without giving notice by mail or otherwise to

the person entitled to it, shall be liable to pay a fine not exceeding twenty-five dollars, to be imposed by the proper court-martial on the complaint of any officer interested. In addition to the penalties imposed by any of the provisions of this act every commissioned and non-commissioned officer, musician and private of a company or troop, or any other person who shall appear at any parade or encampment wearing any personal disguise or other unusual or ludicrous article of dress, or any arms, weapons or other implements not required by law, and calculated to excite ridicule or to interrupt the orderly and peaceable discharge of duty by those under arms, shall be liable to a fine of not more than twenty-five and not less than five dollars, to be imposed by the proper court-martial. <small>Wearing fantastical dress, how punished.</small>

§ 222. The court-martial by which any delinquent is tried may excuse such delinquent, if it shall be made satisfactorily to appear to the court that he has a reasonable excuse for such delinquency. <small>Court-martial may excuse for cause.</small>

§ 223. No action shall be maintained against any member of a court-martial, or officer, or agent, acting under its authority, on account of the imposition of a fine, or the execution of a sentence on any person, if such person shall have been returned as a delinquent and duly summoned, and shall have neglected to appear and render his excuse for such delinquency, or show his exemption before such court. <small>No action can be maintained in case delinquent has been fined by default.</small>

§ 224. When a suit or proceeding shall be commenced in any court by any person against any officer of this state for any act done by such officer in his official capacity, in the discharge of any duty under this act, or against any person acting under authority or order of any such officer, or by virtue of any warrant issued by him pursuant to law, or against any collector or receiver of taxes, the defendant may require the plaintiff in such suit to file security for the payment of the costs that may be incurred by the defendant in such suit or proceeding, and the defendant, in all cases, may plead the general issue, and give the special matter in evidence, and in case the plaintiff shall be non-prossed or non-suited, or have a verdict or judgment against him, the defendant shall recover treble costs. <small>Rules in respect to action at law, when commenced.</small>

OF THE COLLECTION OF FINES AND PENALTIES.

Fines, how collected.

§ 225. For the purpose of collecting such fines as may be imposed by any court-martial authorized by this act, the president of the court shall, within thirty days after the fines have been imposed, make a list of all the persons fined, designating the company to which they respectively belong, and the sums imposed as fines on each person, and shall draw his warrant under his hand and seal, directed to any marshal, sheriff or constable of any city or county (as the case may be), thereby commanding him to levy such fine or fines, together with his costs, of the goods and chattels of such delinquents; and if any such delinquent shall be under age, and live with his father or mother, master or mistress, then to levy such fine or fines with the costs of the goods and chattels of such father and mother, master or mistress, as the case may be; no property now exempt by law shall be exempt from the payment of such fines, and in case the goods and chattels of any delinquent, or the goods and chattels of the father or mother, master or mistress, of any delinquent under age, cannot be found, wherewith to satisfy the same, then to take the body of such delinquent and convey him to the jail of the city or county wherein he shall reside.

Imprisonment for non-payment.

Duty of jailer.

§ 226. It shall be the duty of the jailer to whom such delinquent may be delivered, to keep him closely confined, without bail or mainprize, for two days, for any fine not exceeding two dollars, and two additional days for every dollar above that sum, unless the fine, together with the costs and the jailer's fees, shall be sooner paid.

Warrant for collection of fines may be executed in all parts of the state.

§ 227. Every such marshal, sheriff or constable, to whom any such list and warrant shall be directed and delivered, may execute the same by levying and collecting the fines, or by taking the body of the delinquent in any city, town or county in this state, and shall make return thereof within forty days from the receipt of such warrant, to the officers who issue the same.

Warrant may be renewed.

§ 228. If the marshal, sheriff or constable, shall not be able to collect the fines or take the bodies, within the forty days aforesaid, then the officers issuing the warrant may, at any time thereafter within two years from the time of imposing the fines, issue a new warrant against any delinquent, or renew the former warrant, from time to time, as may become necessary.

§ 229. Any warrant for the collection of fines, issued by virtue of this chapter, shall and may be renewed in the same manner that executions issued from justices' courts may by law be renewed.

§ 230. The amount of any fines so collected shall be paid, by the officer collecting the same, into the county treasury, and shall form a portion of, and be credited to, the regimental fund of the regiment to which the person so fined belonged. *Fines to be paid into the county treasury.*

§ 231. In addition to the bond now required by law to be given by the marshal, sheriff, constable or other officers, for the faithful discharge of his duties, such named officers shall execute a bond for the payment of all moneys by them collected, under the provisions of this act; and the sureties of such officers, hereby authorized to collect fines and penalties, shall be liable for any official delinquency under this act, such bonds to be approved by the county judge of each county. *New bonds to be given by marshal or other officer.*

GENERAL PROVISIONS APPLICABLE TO ALL COURTS-MARTIAL AND COURTS OF INQUIRY.

§ 232. The president of every court-martial, and of every court of inquiry, both before and after he shall have been sworn, and also the judge-advocate, if required, shall issue subpœnas for all witnesses whose attendance at such court may, in his opinion, be necessary in behalf of the people of this state, and also on application for all witnesses in behalf of any officer charged or accused, or persons returned as delinquent; and may direct the commandant of any company to cause such subpœna to be served on any witness or member of his company. *President and judge-advocate may issue subpœnas.*

§ 233. The president of such court-martial, or the court of inquiry, shall have power to administer the usual oath to witnesses, and shall have the same power to compel attending witnesses to be sworn and testify, and to preserve order, as courts of common law jurisdiction; and all sheriffs, jailers and constables, are hereby required to execute any precept issued by such president or court for that purpose. *President to have power to administer oaths and compel attendance of witnesses.*

§ 234. Every witness not appearing in obedience to such subpœna when duly served personally with a copy of the *Penalty for not appearing when*

52 THE MILITIA LAW

summoned as a witness. — same, and not having a sufficient or reasonable excuse, shall forfeit to the people of this state a sum not less than ten nor more than fifty dollars; and the president of such court shall, from time to time, report to the district attorney the names of all such delinquent witnesses, together with the names and places of residence of the persons serving such subpœna, the better to enable him to prosecute for such forfeiture.

President of court-martial to have power to issue attachments to compel witnesses to attend. — § 235. Whenever it shall appear to the satisfaction of any court-martial or court of inquiry, by proof made before such court, that any person duly subpenaed to appear as a witness before said court, shall have refused or neglected, without just cause, to attend as such witness, in conformity to such subpœna, and the party in whose behalf such witness shall have been subpenaed shall make oath that the testimony of such witness is material, such court, or the president thereof, shall have power to issue an attachment to compel the attendance of such witness.

Attachment, how executed. — § 236. Every such attachment shall be executed in the same manner as a warrant, and by any officer authorized to execute warrants, and the fees of the officers serving the same shall be paid by the person against whom the same shall have been issued, unless he shall show reasonable cause, to the satisfaction of such court, for his omission to attend; such costs shall be ascertained by the court, who may thereupon issue an execution for the collection against the person liable to pay the same, and which may be collected as other executions are collected, and by any officer authorized to collect executions issued from courts of justice.

Disorderly conduct at court-martial, how punished. — § 237. Any person or persons who shall be guilty of disorderly, contemptuous or insolent behavior in, or use any insulting or contemptuous or indecorous language or expressions to, or before any court-martial or court of inquiry, or any member of either of such courts, in open court, intending to intercept the proceedings or to impair the respect, the authority of such courts, may be committed to the jail of the county in which said courts shall sit, by warrant under the hand and seal of the president of such court.

Warrant for disorderly person, form of. — § 238. Such warrant shall be directed to the sheriff or any or either of the constables and marshals of any such county, or any officer attending the court, and shall set forth the particular circumstances of the offense adjudged to have been committed; and shall command the officer to whom it is directed to take the body of such person and commit him to the jail of the county, there to remain without bail or mainprize, in close confinement for a time to be limited not exceeding three days, and until the officer's fees for committing and the jailer's fees be paid.

§ 239. Such sheriff shall receive the body of any person who shall be brought to him by virtue of such warrant, and keep him until the expiration of the time mentioned in the warrant, and until the officer's and jailer's fees shall be paid, or until the offender shall be discharged by due course of law, unless sooner discharged by any judge of a court of record, in the same manner and under the same rules as in cases of imprisonment under process for contempt from a court at law. *Sheriff to receive body of person arrested.*

§ 240. In the absence of the president of any court-martial, the senior officer present may preside, with all the powers of the president; and all the members of such court shall, when on duty, be in full uniform. *In absence of president, senior officer to preside.*

§ 241. The president of any court-martial or any court of inquiry may appoint, by warrant under his hand and seal, one or more marshals. *President to appoint marshals.*

§ 242. The marshals so appointed may not only perform the usual duties of such marshals, but may also execute all process lawfully issued by such president or court, and perform all acts and duties in this act imposed on and authorized to be performed by any sheriff, marshal or constable. *Duties of marshals.*

§ 243. Whenever the sentence of any court-martial shall be appealed from, the officer hearing the appeal shall require the court, or the president thereof, to furnish him forthwith with a statement of the case, and of the evidence touching the same; which statement and evidence shall, in case of an appeal to the commanding officer of the brigade, be forthwith, on notice of such appeal, transmitted to him. *Statement of case on appeal from sentence to be furnished to officer hearing appeal.*

§ 244. Such statement being furnished, the officer hearing the appeal may hear such further evidence, by affidavit or otherwise, as the nature of the case may require, and for that purpose he shall have power to administer the usual oaths to witnesses produced before him, except in *Further evidence may be taken by officer hearing appeal in certain cases.*

cases where trials may have been had upon charges preferred.

§ 245. The last two sections shall extend to appeals made from the order of an officer approving the sentence of a court-martial.

New warrant for collection of fines may be issued.

§ 246. If any officer having a warrant for the collection of any fine shall not be able to collect the fine within the time specified therein, then the officers issuing the warrant may, at any time thereafter, within two years from the time of imposing the fines, issue a new warrant against any delinquent, or renew the former warrant, from time to time, as may become necessary.

Warrants for collection of fines may be renewed.

§ 247. Any warrant for the collection of fines, issued by virtue of this act, shall and may be renewed in the same manner that executions, issued from justices' courts may by law be renewed.

Presidents of courts-martial to prosecute sheriffs, marshals, &c.

§ 248. It shall be the duty of the respective presidents of courts-martial to prosecute, in the name of the People of the State of New York, any marshal, or constable, sheriff, and their sureties, who shall incur any penalty for neglect in the execution or return of any warrant, or in paying over moneys collected by him.

President of court-martial composed of one person.

§ 249. Whenever any court-martial shall consist of one person, he shall be deemed the president thereof, within the meaning of this act.

Courts-martial for trial of officers absent from parades, how composed and course of procedure in such courts.

§ 250. The chiefs of the staff in each division, regiment or battalion, shall, on or before the first day of November, in each year, return to the commandants of division and brigade, respectively, the names of all commissioned officers absent from any parade, encampment, or drill, which they shall be required by law to attend. Within ten days after the receipt of such returns, the respective commandants of division or brigade, as the case may be, shall order a court-martial, to consist of three commissioned officers, without regard to rank, to pass upon such delinquency. It shall not be necessary to cause the arrest of such absentee, nor to serve any charges, unless, in the discretion of the officer ordering the court, it may be proper; but the delinquent may be fined, pursuant to the provisions of this act, provided notice of the return and of the time appointed for holding the court-martial shall have been delivered to him or left at his usual place of abode, at least ten days before the assembling of said court.

§ 251. The court may excuse any delinquent for good cause shown. *Court may excuse delinquent.*

§ 252. Any fine for offenses against the by-laws of any company of the national guards or of regimental boards, not exceeding the sum of twenty-five dollars, a certified copy of the proceedings relating to the infliction of which has been returned to any regimental court-martial or court of appeals, may be enforced by such court in the manner hereinbefore provided, due notice being given to the delinquent; and further provided that a certified copy of said by-laws be filed with the commandant of the regiment. *Court-martial may collect company fines.*

§ 253. Whenever any portion of the military forces of this state shall be ordered to assemble for purposes of military instruction, under the authority of the commander-in-chief, or whenever any part of the state forces shall be ordered to assemble, under his authority, in time of war, insurrection, invasion, or public danger, the rules and articles of war, and general regulations for the government of the army of the United States, so far as they are applicable, and with such modifications as the commander-in-chief may prescribe, shall be considered in force and regarded as a part of this act, during the continuance of such instruction, and to the close of such state of war, invasion, insurrection, or public danger; but no punishment under such rules and articles which shall extend to the taking of life, shall, in any case, be inflicted, except in time of actual war, invasion or insurrection, declared by proclamation of the governor to exist. *Articles of war and army regulations to be in force in certain cases.*

OF THE DUTIES OF CERTAIN STAFF OFFICERS, AND OF VARIOUS MATTERS CONNECTED WITH THEIR VARIOUS RESPECTIVE DEPARTMENTS.

Of the Adjutant-General.

§ 254. The adjutant-general shall keep a roster of all the officers of the military forces of this state, containing the date of their commissions, their ranks, the corps to which they belong, the division, brigade and regiment of such corps, and the places of their residence, as accurately as can be ascertained; which roster shall be revised and corrected every year. *Adjutant-general to keep roster.*

§ 255. He shall also enter in a book, to be kept for that purpose, a local description of the several company, regimental, brigade and division districts.

He shall enter in a book descriptions of districts.

§ 256. It shall be the duty of the commandants of divisions and brigades to furnish the adjutant-general with a roster of their officers, containing the facts requisite to enable him to comply with the provisions of this act.

Commandants to furnish roster.

§ 257. The books required by the adjutant-general to comply with this act, shall be furnished him at the expense of this state, and shall go to his successors in office.

Books to be furnished.

§ 258. The seal now used in the office of the adjutant-general shall continue to be the seal of his office, and shall from time to time be delivered to his successor in office; and all copies of records or papers in his office, duly certified and authenticated under the said seal, shall be evidence in all cases, in like manner as if the originals were produced.

Official seal.

§ 259. It shall be the duty of the adjutant-general to cause so much of the militia laws as shall at any time be in force to be printed in proper form, from time to time, and to distribute one copy to each commissioned officer, and to each town clerk, supervisors' clerk, and county treasurer in this state; and also, to prepare and cause all necessary blank books, forms and notices to be transmitted at the expense of this state, to carry into full effect the provisions of this act; and the comptroller is hereby directed to draw his warrant on the treasurer of this state for the expenses incurred under this section.

Adjutant-general to cause militia laws to be published and distributed.

§ 260. The adjutant-general is hereby authorized to appoint an assistant, who shall have the rank of colonel, and be commissioned by the commander-in-chief, and who shall hold such office during the pleasure of the adjutant-general. In the absence of the adjutant-general from the city of Albany, or in case of his inability to perform his duties, his assistant shall have full power to perform all the duties appertaining to the office of adjutant-general. But nothing in this section shall be so construed as to give any validity to the acts of said assistant, in case of the disapproval of the adjutant-general.

Assistant-adjutant-general.

Of the Commissary-General.

§ 261. The commissary-general shall keep in good repair the arsenals and magazines of the state, and attend to the due preservation and safe keeping, cleaning and repairing, of the ordnance, arms, accoutrements, ammunition, munitions of war, and implements of every description, the property of this state; and he shall at all times have the control and disposition of the same for that purpose. <small>Commissary-general, his duties.</small>

§ 262. He shall, under the direction of the commander-in-chief, dispose to the best advantage of all damaged powder, and of all ordnance, arms, ammunition, accoutrements, tools, implements, and warlike stores of every kind whatsoever, that shall be deemed unsuitable for the use of the state. <small>Sale of damaged arms, &c.</small>

§ 263. He shall, from time to time, render a just and true account of all sales made by him, with all convenient speed, to the governor, and shall pay the proceeds of such sale into the treasury of the state for military purposes, or expend the same in the purchase of suitable arms, ammunition, and camp or other equipage, as the commander-in-chief may direct. <small>Report to commander-in-chief.</small>

§ 264. Whenever the commanding officer of a brigade shall certify that a stand of colors, or any drums, fifes or bugles, are necessary for any company, battalion or regiment in his brigade, the commissary-general, with the approbation of the commander-in-chief, shall furnish such company, battalion or regiment, with a stand of colors, and a sufficiency of drums, fifes and bugles, at the expense of the state. <small>Colors, bugles, &c., to be furnished.</small>

§ 265. The commissary-general shall issue the proper allowance of powder and balls to artillery companies for practice; and the several commandants of artillery companies shall annually report to the commissary-general the situation and state of the pieces of ordnance, arms, implements and accoutrements, the property of the state, entrusted to their charges respectively. <small>Ammunition to be furnished.</small>

§ 266. The commissary-general shall issue all ammunition, suited to the several arms of the service, upon the requisition of any commandant of brigade, regiment or battalion; and shall, on a like requisition, replace such articles or implements for ordnance, as may be by use rendered unfit for service.

§ 267. The commissary-general shall report annually to the commander-in-chief, whose duty it shall be to transmit <small>Annual report.</small>

the same to the legislature, a true and particular statement, showing the actual situation and disposition of all the ordnance, arms, ammunition and other munitions of war, property or things, which in any wise appertain to or respect the department confided to his keeping.

<small>Accurate accounts to be kept.</small>

§ 268. He shall keep a just and true account of all the expenses necessarily incurred in and about his department, which shall include all expenses for transportation to and from the arsenals, all ordnance, arms, ammunition and camp equipage, and deliver the same to the comptroller, who shall thereupon examine and audit the same, and shall draw his warrant on the treasurer for such sum as he shall audit and certify to be due.

<small>Judge-advocate-general to prosecute bonds.</small>

§ 269. It shall be the duty of the judge-advocate-general to prosecute any bond, the condition of which is violated by a neglect or refusal of any officer to report the condition of any arms or equipage, or to return the same to any of the arsenals of this state, as required by law.

<small>Assistant commissary-general.</small>

§ 270. The commissary-general is authorized to appoint an assistant, with the rank of colonel, who shall be commissioned by the commander-in-chief, and hold his office during the pleasure of the commissary-general, and shall perform the duties now required by law to be performed by the military storekeeper at the New York arsenal, and shall be compensated in the same manner as such military storekeeper has been compensated. In the absence of the commissary-general from the city of New York, or in case of his inability to perform his duties, his assistant shall have full power to perform all the duties appertaining to the office of the commissary-general; but nothing in this section shall be so construed as to give any validity to the acts of such assistant in case of the disapproval of the commissary-general.

Of the Inspector-General.

<small>Inspector-general to visit regimental districts, inspect armories, &c.</small>

§ 271. It shall be the duty of the inspector-general to visit, at least once in every two years, each regimental district in the state. He shall critically inspect, as often as he may deem necessary, every branch connected with the military service, including armories, arsenals and military storehouses; and he shall also attend to the organization of the militia, and report to general head-quarters the

OF THE STATE OF NEW YORK. 59

improvement in discipline and tactical instruction of the uniformed forces.

§ 272. Commandants of regiments and companies shall furnish to the inspector-general such information as he may require, as to the number and kind of arms, equipments and military property of the state issued to their respective regiments and companies; and, at the conclusion of the inspection of any armory, arsenal or military storehouse, if he find the property which ought to be kept therein, or any part of it, missing, injured, unfit for use, or deficient in any respect, he shall forthwith report the facts, in respect thereto, to the commander-in-chief. *Commandants to report to him number of arms, &c.*

§ 273. It shall be his duty, after the first day in November in each year, to inspect the tents and camp equipage belonging to the state, and report any deficiency therein to the commander-in-chief, on or before the first day of January thereafter. *Inspector of camp equipage.*

§ 274. In his annual report he shall state what general and field officers have been in command of parades and encampments, what changes of general or field officers have been made, and what degree of improvement has been attained by both officers and men, and whether the general regulations have been observed, together with such suggestions as he may see fit to make. *To report number of encampments, &c.*

§ 275. To the inspector-general will be referred, by order of the commander-in-chief, such matters as require an examination at a distance from the general head-quarters, for the information of the commander-in-chief; and it shall be the duty of inspector-general, upon such reference, to report upon the qualifications of persons named, to the commander-in-chief, for appointment to military office, and also upon the possession of the necessary requisites by the applicants for the organization of companies. *Matters at a distance and questions as to qualifications for military office to be referred to inspector-general.*

§ 276. The division and brigade inspectors, whenever required by the inspector-general, shall report to him the condition of their respective divisions or brigades, and shall also, upon his request, report to him upon any matter properly belonging to his department, which may require examination within their respective division or brigade districts. *Division and brigade inspectors to report to him.*

§ 277. The inspector-general shall visit the several encampments which shall be ordered by the commander-in- *Inspector-general shall visit camps.*

chief and to ascertain whether the troops have been properly instructed in the exercises and evolutions of the field; he will cause them to be exercised in the manœuvres required to be practised during the year, as prescribed by the regulations; and he will give his instructions, as to the exercises, to the commanding officer, who will issue all necessary orders and directions to the troops for their execution.

The inspector-general shall once in every two years examine books and accounts of military boards.

§ 278. The inspector-general shall, at least once in every two years, examine the book of proceedings of the board of auditors of each regiment, and the accounts filed with the secretary of such board during the two years previous, or since his last examination made by the inspector-general, and he shall carefully compare the book of proceedings with accounts; he shall also examine the warrants drawn by the board of auditors, in the possession of the county treasurer, and he shall specially report to the commander-in-chief whether the proceedings of the board of auditors are regularly and properly entered, and whether the warrants are in due form; and whether any military funds have been drawn from the county treasury for improper purposes, or by persons not entitled thereto.

Assistant inspector-general.

§ 279. The inspector-general is hereby authorized to appoint an assistant, who shall have the rank of colonel, and be commissioned by the commander-in-chief, and who shall hold such office during the pleasure of the inspector-general, and shall receive the same compensation as the assistant adjutant-general. In the absence of the inspector-general from the city of Albany, or in case of his inability to perform his duties, his assistant shall have full power to perform all duties appertaining to the office of the inspector-general. But nothing in this section shall be so construed as to give any validity to the acts of said assistant, in case of the disapproval of the inspector-general.

Of the Judge-Advocate-General.

Duties of judge-advocate-general.

§ 280. The judge-advocate-general, as chief of his department, is charged with the supervision, care and management of all things relating to the administration of justice among the military forces of this state. He shall diligently scrutinize and examine the proceedings of all courts-martial where an appeal has been taken, and report thereon for the information of the commander-in-chief; he shall also, in like manner, report in all cases of disputed elections where an appeal has been taken. Under the orders of the commander-in-chief, the judge-advocate-general shall act as judge-advocate at any court-martial where the public interests shall require his attendance.

§ 281. The judge-advocate-general is the legal adviser of the several staff departments, upon all legal questions which may arise therein, and to him may be referred for supervision all contracts, agreements, or other instruments, to be drawn or executed in the course of the business of such department. *The judge-advocate-general the legal adviser of the departments.*

§ 282. The officers of the judge-advocate-general's department, when not engaged in the special duties of the same, may be detailed for such other staff duty as the commandants of their respective brigades or divisions shall direct. *Officers may be detailed.*

OF INVASION, INSURRECTION, BREACHES OF THE PEACE, AND DRAFTS OF THE MILITIA.

Of Invasion and Insurrection.

§ 283. In cases of insurrection or invasion, or imminent danger thereof, the commander-in-chief may, by proclamation or otherwise, order and direct the commandants of such company districts as he shall designate, to accept sufficient volunteers, should the same offer, to raise said company, and maintain the same at the maximum number provided by law, and if sufficient volunteers should not offer, then a sufficient number shall be drafted from the reserve militia of said districts in the manner hereinafter provided, who shall thereupon be enrolled as national guards in said company, and shall be liable to duty in case the military forces of the state should be called into service. *In case of invasion or insurrection companies to be filled by drafting, such drafts to be made from the reserve militia.*

§ 284. The commander-in-chief shall have power, in case of insurrection or invasion, or imminent danger thereof, to order into the service of the state such number and description of companies or regiments of the national guard, or of other militia of the state as he shall deem proper, and under the command of such officers as he shall direct, and in such case the forces so called into service shall receive the same pay and rations as troops in the service of the United States. And all the acts, proclamations and orders *Commander-in-chief to order national guard and other militia into service in certain cases. Acts of governor since April 16th, 1861, confirmed.*

of the governor of this state since the sixteenth day of April, eighteen hundred and sixty-one, relating to the calling out of the militia or volunteers from this state for the service of the United States, are hereby approved, and in all respects legalized and made valid, to the same intent and with the same effect as if they had been issued and done with the previous express authority and direction of the legislature of this state, and all commissions issued or hereafter to be issued to the officers of such volunteer forces by the governor of this state, in accordance with the act of congress in such cases made and provided, are hereby confirmed.

Duty of commandants in case of invasion.

§ 285. In case of any invasion, or of imminent danger thereof, within the limits of any division, brigade, regiment or battalion, it shall be the duty of the commandant of such division, brigade, regiment or battalion to order out, for the defense of the state, the militia, or any part thereof, under his command, and immediately report what he has done to the commander-in-chief, through the adjutant-general.

Notice of invasion to be given to commander-in-chief.

§ 286. It shall also be his duty to give immediate notice of such invasion, and of the circumstances attending the same, to his immediate commanding officer, by whom such information shall be transmitted, with the utmost expedition to the commander-in-chief.

Duty of commandants in case of insurrection.

§ 287. The commandant of every regiment or battalion, within the limits of which an insurrection may happen, shall immediately assemble his regiment or battalion, under arms, and with the utmost expedition shall transmit information of such insurrection to the commandant of his brigade and to the commander-in-chief.

Notice to be given to county judge.

§ 288. He shall also give immediate notice of such insurrection to any judge of the county in which it shall happen, and shall take such measures for its suppression as to such judge shall appear most proper and effectual.

Duty of county judge in case of insurrection.

§ 289. If the said judge shall deem a greater force requisite to quell the insurrection, he shall require such additional force as he may deem necessary from the commandant of the division, or of any brigade therein, whose duty it shall be to obey his requisition.

Persons wounded in the service of the state

§ 290. Every person who, whilst in the actual service of this state, shall be wounded or disabled in opposing or

OF THE STATE OF NEW YORK. 63

suppressing any invasion or insurrection, shall be taken care of and provided for at the expense of the state. *to be provided for.*

OF RIOTS, TUMULTS, BREACHES OF THE PEACE AND RESISTANCE TO PROCESS.

§ 291. In case of any breach of the peace, tumult, riot or resistance to process of this state, or apprehension of imminent danger of the same, it shall be lawful for the sheriff of any county, or the mayor of any city, to call for aid from any division, brigade, regiment, battalion or company; and it shall be the duty of the commanding officer of such division, brigade, regiment, battalion or company, to whom such order is given, to order out, in aid of the civil authorities, the military force, or any part thereof under his command. *In case of riot, sheriff or mayor may call for aid from military forces.*

§ 292. In such case it shall not be necessary for commandants of companies to issue written orders or notices for calling out their men, but verbal orders and notices shall be sufficient. *In case of riot, verbal orders sufficient.*

§ 293. It shall be the duty of the commanding officer of any division, brigade, regiment, battalion or company, in all cases when so called into service, to provide the men of his command, so ordered out, with at least twenty-four rounds of ball cartridge, and arms in complete order for actual service. *Forces to be furnished with 24 rounds of ball cartridge.*

§ 294. Such officer shall be subject, as provided by law, to the sheriff or public officer who shall so require his aid; and for refusing or neglecting to obey the order of such sheriff, or public officer so requiring service, or for interfering or in any way hindering or preventing the men of his command from performing such duty, or in any manner, by neglect or delay, preventing the due execution of law, every such commanding officer, and every commissioned officer under his command so offending, shall be liable to a fine of not less than one hundred nor more than five hundred dollars, and imprisonment in the county jail for a period not exceeding six months. *Military officers to be subject to orders of sheriff, penalty for neglect of duty.*

§ 295. It shall be the duty of the district attorney of any county where such offense shall be committed, to prosecute the same; and in addition thereto, such officer shall be liable to be tried by court-martial and sentenced to be *Duty of district attorney.*

cashiered and incapacitated forever after for holding military commission in this state.

Further penalties.

§ 296. Any non-commissioned officer, musician or private, who shall neglect or refuse to obey the orders of his commanding officer in the case above provided for, shall be liable to a fine of not less than twenty-five nor more than one hundred dollars, and imprisonment in the county jail for a period not to exceed three months, to be prosecuted and recovered in the manner hereinbefore provided in the case of commissioned officers.

In case of riot, forces to receive certain compensation; those injured to be provided for.

§ 297. All officers, non-commissioned officers and privates, in cases of riot, tumult, breach of the peace, resistance to process, or whenever called upon in aid of the civil authorities, shall receive the compensation provided by an act entitled, "An Act to enforce the laws and preserve order," passed April 15th, eighteen hundred and forty-five, which continues in force and shall be published with this act; and every person who shall be wounded or disabled in such service, shall be taken care of and provided for at the expense of the county where such service shall be rendered.

OF DRAFTS OF THE MILITIA.

Drafts, how made.

§ 298. Whenever the commander-in-chief shall order a draft from the reserved militia of any company district, to raise the company of the national guard therein to, and maintain the same at, either the minimum or maximum number provided by this act, or whenever a general draft of the militia shall be made by order of the commander-in-chief, or of the president of the United States, such draft shall be determined by lot, to be drawn by the clerk of the county in which such roll has been filed, in the presence of the county judge and the mayor of any city, or the supervisor of any town or ward, upon the requisition of the commanding officer of the regiment within whose bounds such person may reside.

Exemption may be presented to county judge.

§ 299. Any person so drafted may, within five days after receiving notice of the same, present to the county judge of such county his certificate of exemption, or other proof of his non-liability to military duty, which shall be duly verified, and if such county judge shall decide that such person is exempt or not liable, he shall be discharged and another person shall be drafted in his stead, in accordance with the provisions of this act.

§ 300. Any person so drafted, in accordance with the above provisions, may offer a substitute at the time of the rendezvous of the drafted military force and militia, and such substitute, if he shall be an able-bodied man, of the age of twenty-one years and upwards, and shall consent in writing to subject himself to all the duties, fines, forfeitures and punishments to which his principal would have been subject had he personally served, shall be accepted by the commandant of the company of drafted militia to which his principal may belong. *[Person drafted may furnish substitute.]*

§ 301. Whenever the president of the United States or the commander-in-chief shall order a draft from the militia for public service, such draft shall be made in the following manner: *[Drafts, how made.]*

1. When the draft required to be made shall be a number equal to one or more companies to each brigade, such draft shall be made by company, to be determined by lot, to be drawn by the commandant of brigade in the presence of the commanding officers of the regiments composing said brigade from the military forces of the state in his brigade, organized, uniformed, armed and equipped, according to the provisions of this act.

2. In case such draft shall require a number equal to one regiment, such shall be determined by lot in the manner above prescribed.

3. In case such draft shall require a larger number than the whole number of men composing the military force of said brigade, such additional draft shall be made of the requisite number, to supply such deficiency, from the military roll of the reserve militia of each town or ward, filed in the office of the city, village or town clerk, as hereinbefore provided.

§ 302. The commander-in-chief shall prescribe such rules, orders and regulations, relative to the distribution of arms, ammunition and military stores, to the militia when called into actual service, as he may deem proper. *[Distribution of arms.]*

§ 303. The command of any military force, called into service under the provisions of this title, shall devolve upon the senior officer of such force, unless otherwise specially ordered by the commander-in-chief. *[Command to devolve on senior officer.]*

OF THE MILITARY FUND OF THE STATE, AND APPROPRIATIONS FOR MILITARY PURPOSES.

Military fund to be kept separate.

§ 804. The moneys received from the several county treasurers, under the provisions of this act, shall be kept separate and apart from the current and ordinary finances of this state, and shall be applied to the purposes mentioned in this act and to no other.

Appropriation for military purposes.

§ 305. For the purchase of uniforms and equipments, pay of officers and privates, and other expenditures authorized by this act, the sum of three hundred thousand dollars is hereby appropriated from the moneys mentioned in the last preceding section, and from any other moneys in the treasury not otherwise appropriated.

MISCELLANEOUS PROVISIONS.

Commander-in-chief may establish rules and regulations.

§ 306. The commander-in-chief is hereby authorized to establish and prescribe such rules, regulations, forms and precedents as he shall deem proper for the use and government of the military forces of the state, and to carry into full effect the provisions of this act. Such rules, regulations, forms and precedents shall be published in orders by the adjutant-general, and, from time to time, distributed to the commissioned officers of the state.

Certificate to be granted at the end of seven years' service to non-commissioned officers and privates.

§ 307. Whenever any non-commissioned officers, musicians or privates, of any uniform company or troop, shall have performed service in any such company or troop for the space of seven years from the time of his enlistment therein, properly uniformed according to the provisions of law, he shall be furnished, on application, by the commanding officer of such company or troop, with a certificate, duly setting forth such facts, which shall, for all purposes, be deemed *prima facie* evidence thereof.

Commandant of company to deliver such certificates.

§ 308. The commanding officer of every uniform company or troop shall, on the application of any commissioned, non-commissioned officer, musician or private of his company, deliver to him a certificate, stating that such person is a member of his company, and whether he is uniformed according to law, and how recently he may have performed duty in said company. Such certificate, when dated within six months, shall be deemed for all purposes *prima facie* evidence of the matters therein stated.

§ 309. Every officer, non-commissioned officer, musician and private of the uniformed militia of this state, who shall have provided himself with a uniform, arms or accoutrements required by law or regulation, shall hold the same exempt from all suits, distresses, executions or sales for debt, or for the payment of taxes; and every mounted officer, and every member of a troop of cavalry or light artillery, who shall own a suitable horse necessary for his use as such officer or member, shall hold the same with like exemption. Uniform, arms, horses, &c., to be exempt from execution.

§ 310. The rules and regulations, prepared by a board of officers under section one of title nine of the militia law, passed April seventeen, eighteen hundred and fifty-four, with such changes and modifications as are provided in this act, having received the approval of the commander-in-chief are hereby ratified and confirmed; and the commander-in-chief is hereby authorized to make such changes and alterations in said regulations, from time to time, as he may deem expedient. Rules and regulations confirmed.

§ 311. The commandants of regiments may appoint ordnance sergeants as keepers of armories, not exceeding one to each armory, who shall be under the authority and hold office during the pleasure of the commandant; such ordnance sergeants shall be paid as now provided for keepers of armories. Ordnance-sergeants as keepers of armories.

§ 312. No person belonging to the military forces shall be arrested on any civil process while going to, remaining at, or returning from any place at which he may be required to attend for military duty. Arrest, exemption from.

§ 313. Any person who shall purchase, retain, or have in custody or possession without right any military property belonging to this state marked as or known to him to be such, and shall, after proper demand, refuse to deliver the same to any officer entitled to the possession thereof, shall be liable to an action for the recovery of the possession of such military property, and of a penalty of not less than ten nor more than one hundred dollars. Penalty for refusal to deliver state property.

§ 314. Any person belonging to the military forces who shall, contrary to the lawful order of the proper officer, retain in his possession or control any military property of this state, shall be liable to an action to recover the possession thereof and to pay a fine of not less than ten nor more Commanding officers may take possession of state property illegally detained wherever found.

than one hundred dollars, and shall also be deemed guilty of a misdemeanor; and any commanding officer may take possession thereof, or of such military property mentioned in the preceding section wherever the same may be found.

<small>Actions may be brought to recover possession of state property.</small>

§ 315. Actions to recover the possession of military property and the amount of any fine or penalty under the two preceding sections may be brought, by any officer entitled to the possession of such property, in any court of competent jurisdiction, and such fine or penalty together with all other fines or penalties prescribed by this act, and by chapter three hundred and ninety-eight of the Session Laws of eighteen hundred and fifty-four, shall be paid to the treasurer of the county where the offender may reside, for the benefit of the military fund of the regiment located therein. The possession of any military property, or the amount of a fine or penalty, may be recovered in the same action. Proceedings at law shall not preclude the punishment of any military person in the military courts.

<small>Ferries and toll-bridges, free passage over.</small>

§ 316. Any person belonging to the military forces of this state, going to or returning from any parade, encampment, drill or meeting, which he may be required by law to attend, shall, together with his conveyance and the military property of the state, be allowed to pass free through all toll-gates, over toll-bridges and ferries.

<small>Colonelcy by brevet.</small>

§ 317. Whenever any officer shall have served or shall hereafter serve continuously and honorably as commandant of any military company, under a military commission, issued under the laws of this state, for the period of twenty years, the commander-in-chief shall have power to confer upon such officer the brevet or honorary rank of colonel, but such brevet shall not confer additional pay or emoluments for services under this act.

<small>Pay of forces called out to suppress riots, &c.</small>

§ 318. All officers, non-commissioned officers, musicians and privates of the national guard, while on duty or assembled therefor, pursuant to the order of the sheriff of any county, or the mayor of any city, in cases of riot, tumult, breach of peace, resistance to process, or whenever called upon in aid of the civil authorities, shall receive the compensation provided by the twenty-first section of the act entitled "An act to enforce the laws and preserve order," passed April fifteen, eighteen hundred and forty-five, and such compensation shall be audited, allowed and paid by the supervisors of the county where such service is rendered, and shall be a portion of the county charges of said county, to be levied and raised as other county charges are levied and raised.

§ 319. Chapter three hundred and ninety-eight of the Laws of eighteen hundred and fifty-four, except such parts of the same as are referred to in sections five and ten of this title, chapters two hundred and sixty-one and five hundred and thirty-six of the Laws of eighteen hundred and fifty-five, chapters one hundred and twenty-nine and three hundred and forty-three of the Laws of eighteen hundred and fifty-eight, and all other acts and parts of acts conflicting with this act are hereby repealed; but such repeal shall not affect any legal proceedings commenced under them. *Repeal of inconsistent acts.*

§ 320. This act shall take effect immediately.

STATE OF NEW YORK,
OFFICE OF THE SECRETARY OF STATE.

I have compared the preceding with the original law on file in this office, and do certify that the same is a correct transcript therefrom and of the whole of said original.

HORATIO BALLARD,
Secretary of State.

STATE OF NEW YORK,
GENERAL HEADQUARTERS.

ALBANY, *May* 29, 1862.

GENERAL ORDERS,
No. 34.

The Commander-in-Chief hereby establishes the following forms and precedents for the use of the Militia of this State, in accordance with the provisions of an act entitled "An act to provide for the enrollment of the Militia, the organization and discipline of the National Guard of the State of New York, and for the public defence," passed April 23d, 1862, which act is hereby published and promulgated for the information and government of the Militia of this State.

By order of the Commander-in-Chief.

THOS. HILLHOUSE,
Adjutant-General.

FORMS.

(No. 1.)
ENROLLMENT

Of persons liable to Military duty in the District of.........,
Company ...., ... Regiment, County of ....,
Colonel commanding, ...

Four copies of this enrollment shall be made by the enrolling officers, one of which shall be filed in the office of the town or city clerk, or of the county clerk, if there be no town or city clerk, on or before July 1st, one shall be retained by him, and the remaining two shall be filed after being corrected, by striking out the names of exempts, the one in the office of the Adjutant-General, and the other in the office of the county clerk of the county in which the company district is situated. *Militia Law*, § 4.

Name.	Residence.	Age.	Class.

...., *Enrolling Officer.*

(No. 2.)
CERTIFICATE THAT ENROLLMENT HAS BEEN FILED.
Militia Law, § 4.

I do hereby certify that a copy of an enrollment of persons liable to military duty in .... Company District, ... Regiment, County of ...., was duly filed in my office on the ...... day of ...., by ...., Enrolling officer.

Dated ....

(No. 3.)
NOTICE OF FILING OF ENROLLMENT.

To be published by the Clerk of the Board of Supervisors once a week for four weeks previous to the first. day of August, in a newspaper published in the county.
Militia Law, § 8.

Notice is hereby given that the enrollments of persons liable to military duty in the several company districts of this county, have been completed and filed in the offices of the several town clerks therein (or in the office of the city or county clerk), and that any person who claims that he is, for any reason, exempt, shall, on or before the fifteenth day of August next, file a written statement of such exemption in such office, verified by affidavit, in default of which such person shall lose the benefit of such exemption.

Dated ....
 ...., *Clerk of Board of Supervisors,*
 County of ....

(No. 4.)
FORM OF VERIFICATION OF EXEMPTION.

COUNTY OF ...., ss.

...., being duly sworn, doth depose and say that he is the same person named in the foregoing statement of exemption, and that the matters therein stated, upon which his claim for exemption from military duty is founded, are true.

 ....

Sworn to before me, this ...... day
of ...., 18 ..

 ....

FORMS AND INSTRUCTIONS.

(No. 5.)
FORM OF COMPANY ROLL FOR INFANTRY OR RIFLEMEN.
NATIONAL GUARD STATE OF NEW YORK.

Roll of the Company of .... in the .... Regiment, ... Brigade, and .... Division of .... the National Guard of the State of New York, under the command of Captain ...., as corrected on the ....

Names of Commissioned Officers.	Drums.	Fifes.	Bugles.	Rifles.	Muskets.	Bayonets.	Cartridge Boxes.	Steel Rods.	Scabbard and Belts.	Flints.	Wires and Brushes.	Worms.	Knapsacks.	Pouches.	Powder Horns.	Cartridge with Balls.	Loose Balls.	Pounds of Powder.	Haversacks.	Canteens.	REMARKS.
Names of Non-Commissioned Officers. { Musicians. Corporals. Sergeants.																					
Names of Privates.																					

MILITIA LAW

(No. 6.)

FORM OF COMPANY ROLL FOR ARTILLERY.
NATIONAL GUARD, STATE OF NEW YORK.

Roll of the Company of Artillery, in the .... Regiment, ... Brigade, and .... Division of the National Guard of the State of New York, under the command of Captain ...., as corrected on the ....

Names of Commiss'd Officers.	Muskets.	Bayonets.	Cartouch Boxes.	Cartridges with Balls.	Swords and Belts.	Knapsacks.	Uniforms.	Colors.	Brass—Founders.	Iron—Pounders.	Cartridges.	Ammunition Boxes.	Tarpaulins.	Tillers.	Tompions and Straps.	Apron.	Drag Ropes.	Limbers.	Sponges.	Worms and Ladles.	Lintstocks.	Portfire Stocks.	Portfire Cases.	Haversacks.	Powder Horns.	Tube Boxes.	Nippers.	Priming Wires.	Gimlets.	Hammers.	Belts.	Ammunition Carts.	Sets Horse Harness.	Tar Buckets.	Pounds of Powder.	Canister Shot.	Flannel Cartridges.	Port Fire.	Slow Match.	Tubes.	Tumbrils.	Drums.	Fifes.	Haversacks.	Canteens.	REMARKS.
Names Non-commis'd Officers — Sergeants, Corporals, Musicians.																																														
Names of Privates.																																														

FORMS AND INSTRUCTIONS.

(No. 7.)
FORM OF COMPANY ROLL FOR CAVALRY.
NATIONAL GUARD, STATE OF NEW YORK.

Roll of the Company of Cavalry, in the ………… Regiment, ………… Brigade, and ………… Division of the National Guard of the State of New York, under the command of Capt. …………, as corrected on the …………

Names of Commissioned Officers.	Colors.	Uniforms.	Caps.	Pairs Boots.	Pairs Spurs.	Sabres.	Pairs Pistols.	Cartouch Boxes.	Cartridges.	Horses, 14½ hands.	Saddles.	Holsters.	Breast Plates.	Cruppers.	Bridles.	Mail Pillions.	Valises.	Trumpet.	Bugle.	REMARKS.
Names of Non-Commissioned Officers. { Sergeants. { Corporals. { Musicians.																				
Names of Privates.																				

(No. 8.)
FORM OF RESIGNATION.

To ...., *Adjutant-General of the State of New York:*

SIR:

The undersigned would respectfully represent, that he now holds the office of .... in the ...... Regiment, ... Brigade and .... Division of the National Guard of this state, and that in consequence of (*here state the reasons that induce the application for a discharge, particularly*) he is induced to resign said office, and doth hereby resign the same. Your petitioner respectfully represents that he is not under arrest or returned to court-martial for any deficiency or delinquency; and that he has delivered over all moneys, books and other property of the state, in his possession, to the officer authorized by law to receive the same; and your petitioner respectfully solicits that you will be pleased to accept this his said resignation, and grant him a discharge.

....

Dated at ...., this ......
day of ...., A. D., 18..

The resignation of the above named officer is hereby approved (or disapproved for the following reasons):

...., *Brigadier-General Commanding ...... Brigade, National Guard, S. N. Y.*

The commanding officers of Brigades shall receive the resignations of such commissioned officers as may resign in their respective Brigades, and shall transmit the same to the Adjutant-General. Resignations of all other commissioned officers shall be made direct to the commander-in-chief.

(No. 9.)
FORM OF ACCEPTANCE OF RESIGNATION.

SPECIAL ORDERS, No. ....

STATE OF NEW YORK, GENERAL HEADQUARTERS,
Albany, ..., 186..

The commander-in-chief has accepted the resignation of ...., and he is hereby, at his own request, honorably discharged from said office.

By order of the commander-in-chief.

...., *Adjutant-General.*

FORMS AND INSTRUCTIONS. 79

(No. 10.)

Form of Order for Election.

STATE OF NEW YORK, REGIMENTAL ORDERS.

.................., 18..

Pursuant to the provisions of the militia laws of this State, I do hereby order an election to be held to fill the office of .... in the .... regiment, ... brigade, and .... division of the National Guard of this State, which has become vacant by the resignation of .... The time and place of holding said election will, without delay, be appointed by Captain ...., who will cause the proper notices for the same to be duly served on the members of the company under his command.

.... } *and Commanding Officer of Regiment, &c.*

(No. 11.)

Form of Notice for Company Election.

To Sergeant ....

You are hereby ordered to notify the several persons whose names are hereunder written, with three days' notice, that an election will be held on the .... day of ...., at ..... o'clock in the .... noon, at the house of ...., in the town of ...., for the purpose of choosing a suitable person to fill the office of ...., in the .... regiment, ... brigade, and .... division, of the National Guard of the State of New York, which has become vacant by the resignation of .... Hereof fail not; and make due return to me of the time when you shall have respectively notified said persons, and the manner thereof.

Dated at ...., this .... day of ...., A. D. 18 ..

Names.	Time of Serving Notice.	Manner of serving Notice.			
		R.	S.	L.	A.

(No. 12.)

FORM OF SERGEANT'S RETURN OF SERVICE OF NOTICE.

I, the within named Sergeant, ..., do hereby certify that the several persons named in the within notice were duly notified by me, as within directed, at the times and in the manner set opposite to their respective names, that is to say, those marked R, by reading the said notice; those marked S, by stating the substance thereof; those marked L, by leaving a notice thereof, signed by me, at their usual places of abode; and those marked A, by affixing such notice on the outer door of their respective houses.

...., *Sergeant.*

(No. 13.)

CAPTAIN'S CERTIFICATE.

I certify that the above named .... personally appeared before me, on the ...... day ...., A. D. 18 .., and duly made oath to the truth of the above return.

.... } *Captain.*

N. B. A trifling alteration will adapt the above form of order and notice to the election of a general field officer.

(No. 14.)

FORM OF NOTICE TO BE LEFT BY SERGEANT AT THE USUAL PLACE OF ABODE, IN CASE OF ABSENCE.

To Mr. ....

    Sir,

    You are hereby notified that an election will be held on the .... day of ...., at ... o'clock in the .... noon, at the house of ...., in the town of ...., for the purpose of choosing a suitable person to fill the office of .... in the .... regiment, ... brigade, and .... division, of the National Guard of the State of New York, which has become vacant by the resignation of ....

    Dated this ...... day of ...., A. D. 18..

        By order of Captain ....

                .... } *Sergeant.*

(No. 15.)

FORM OF RECORD OF PROCEEDINGS,

To be certified by the presiding officer at an election to the commanding officer of Brigade.

Record of proceedings had at the town of ...., on the .... day of ...., A. D. 18..; for the election of officers to fill vacancies in the .... Regiment, ... Brigade, and .... Division, of the National Guard of the State of New York.

Offices to be filled.	Names of Candidates for each office.	No. of written votes for each Candidate.	Names of persons duly elected	In the room of whom elected, and cause of vacancy.	Place of abode of the persons elected.

I certify the above to be just and true.

.... } *Captain and Presiding Officer.*

(No. 16.)

FORM OF NOTICE TO AN OFFICER ELECT, AND ACCEPTANCE.

To ....
    SIR,

    At an election this day held, in pursuance of the militia laws of this State, at the house of ...., in the town of ...., you were duly chosen to fill the office of .... in the .... regiment, ... brigade, and .... division, of the National Guard of this State. As presiding officer at said election, it becomes my duty to notify you of your election, and to request that you will signify to me your acceptance within ten days after the receipt hereof, otherwise you will be considered as declining.

    Respectfully your obedient servant,

              .... } *and Presiding Officer.*

Dated at ...., this ...... }
  day of ...., A. D. 18... }

    I hereby signify my willingness to serve in the office of ...., to which I have been chosen, as stated in the above notice. Dated at ...., this .... day of ...., A. D. 18..

            .... }

(No. 17.)

FORM OF RETURN OF NON-COMMISSIONED OFFICERS ELECTED, TO BE CERTIFIED BY COMMANDING OFFICERS OF COMPANIES TO COMMANDING OFFICER OF REGIMENT OR SEPARATE BATTALION, IN ORDER THAT WARRANTS MAY BE ISSUED TO THE PERSONS DULY ELECTED.

RETURN of non-commissioned officers elected in the company of ...., under the command of ...., in the .... regiment, ... brigade, and .... division of the National Guard of the State of New York.

	Names of persons elected.	Time when.	Place of abode.	In the room of whom elected and the cause of the vacancy.
Corporals. Sergeants.				

I certify the above return to be true.

.........., ..., *Captain.*

(No. 18.)

FORM OF RETURN OF STAFF OFFICERS APPOINTED,

To be certified by Commandants of Regiments and separate Battalions to Brigadier-General.

Return of Staff Officers appointed in the .... Regiment, ... Brigade, and .... Division, of the National Guard of the State of New York.

Names.	Office.	Corps.	Time when.	Place of abode.	In room of whom appointed, and the cause of vacancy.

I certify the above to be a true return.

.... } *Colonel*

(No 19.)

FORM OF OATH TO BE TAKEN AND SUBSCRIBED BY OFFICERS ON THE RECEIPT OF THEIR COMMISSION.

I .... do solemnly swear (or affirm, as the case may be) that I will support the constitution of the United States and the constitution of the State of New York, and that I will faithfully discharge the duties of the office of .... according to the best of my ability.

Sworn to and subscribed before me, this ...... day of ...., A. D. 18...

.... } *Colonel of* ....
.........*Reg't of* ....

(No. 20.)

FORM OF RETURN OF DELINQUENTS,
Pursuant to § 143, of the Militia Law of 1862.

*A Return of Delinquents and Deficiencies in the Company commanded by ...., in the ....
Regiment of .... of the National Guard of the State of New York, at a parade had at ....,
on the .... day of ...., A. D. 18..*

Names.	Rank.	Statement of Delinquencies.	Penalty.

I certify that the above return is just and true.
Witness my hand, this .... day of ...., A. D. 18..

...., *Captain.*

(No. 21.)

FORM OF A WARRANT TO BE ISSUED BY THE OFFICER HOLDING A COURT-MARTIAL, TO COMMIT A DISORDERLY PERSON.

To all, or any, or either, of the constables or sheriffs of the county of ...., *Greeting:*

Whereas, at a regimental court-martial, this day held at the house of ...., in the town of ...., in pursuance of the militia law of this state, for the trial of all delinquents and deficiencies in the ...... regiment of .... of the National Guard of the State of New York, one .... was in open court guilty of (here state the offense); and whereas, the said court did thereupon adjudge that the said .... should be committed to the jail of the county of ...., there to remain, without bail or mainprize, in close confinement, for the space of ...... day.: These are, therefore, in the name of the People of the State of New York, and by virtue of the said law, to command you forthwith to take the said .... and convey him to the jail of the county of ...., aforesaid; and the sheriff or jailer of said county is hereby empowered and required to receive the body of the said ...., and him safely keep, without bail or mainprize, in close confinement, for the space of .... day., and until your fees and the fees of the said jailer shall be paid, or until he shall be discharged by due course of law.

Given under my hand and seal, in open court, this .... day of ...., A. D., 18...

(No. 22.)

FORM OF WARRANT TO BE ISSUED BY THE OFFICER HOLDING A COURT-MARTIAL, FOR THE COLLECTION OF FINES.

The People of the State of New York, by the grace of God free and independent, to any constable of the county of ...., *Greeting:*

Whereas, at a .... court-martial, held in pursuance of the militia laws of this state, at the house of ...., in the town of ...., on the .... day of ...., for the trial of all delinquents and deficiencies in the .... regiment of .... of the National Guard of the State of New York aforesaid, the several delinquents named in the annexed list were duly fined in sums set opposite to their respective names: These are therefore to command you to levy and collect said fines, together with your costs, according to law, of the goods and chattels of said delinquents; and if any of said delinquents shall be under age, and live with his father or mother, master or mistress, that then you levy and collect the same, together with your costs, as aforesaid, of the goods and chattels of such father or mother, master or mistress, as the case may be ; and in case the goods and chattels of any delinquent, or the goods and chattels of the father or mother, master or mistress of any delinquent under age, cannot be found wherewith to satisfy the same, then that you take the body of the delinquent and convey him to the jail of the county of .... ; and of your doings herein make return to me, within forty days from the day of the date of these presents.

Given under my hand and seal, this ..... day of ...., 18..

.... } *President of said Court.*

(No. 23.)

FORM OF LIST TO BE ANNEXED TO WARRANT TO COLLECT FINES, AND TO BE REPORTED TO THE OFFICER OF THE COURT-MARTIAL.

List of persons fined at a .... Court-Martial, held at the house of ...., in the town of ...., on the .... day of ...., for the trial of all delinquents and deficiencies in the .... Regiment of .... of the National Guard of the State of New York.

Names of Delinquents.	Under 21 years.	Place of abode.	Company to which Delinquents belong.	Amount of Fines imposed.	
				Dollars.	Cents.

Dated at ...., this .... day of ...., 18..

...., Commandant of .... Reg't.

(No. 24.)

FORM OF AN ORDER FOR ARREST.

BRIGADE (DIVISION OR GENERAL) ORDER.

HEADQUARTERS OF THE (BRIGADE OR DIVISION) OF
THE NATIONAL GUARD OF THE STATE OF NEW YORK.

[Here insert the place and date.]

To ....

You are hereby forthwith directed to repair to the quarters of .... (here insert the regiment, brigade and division) of the militia of the State of New York: You will then and there cause the said officer to be arrested, by reading this warrant to him, or leaving a certified copy thereof at his quarters, that. the said .... may be brought to answer certain charges and specifications of unmilitary conduct. Of your doings hereof make due return to me without unnecessary delay.

...., *General, &c.*

(No. 25.)

FORM OF AN ORDER DIRECTED TO AN ARRESTED OFFICER, COMMANDING HIM TO DELIVER BOOKS, PAPERS, &C.

HEADQUARTERS, &c.

...... Orders.   [Insert place and date.]

To ....

Sir: You are hereby directed forthwith to deliver all books, papers, moneys and other property in your possession, belonging to the (regiment, brigade or division,) to ...., to the end that the same may be held by him, the said ...., until the charges on which you have been arrested shall have been investigated.

...., *General.*
...., *Aid-de-Camp.*

(No. 26.)

FORM OF WARRANT TO PERSON APPOINTED MARSHAL, TO BE GRANTED BY THE PRESIDENT OF A COURT-MARTIAL.

To ....

You having been appointed marshal for (division or brigade, as the case may be) court-martial, for the trial of A. B., of the ...... regiment, of the ...... brigade, of the ...... division of the National Guard of the State of New York, I do therefore, by virtue of the power in me vested as president of the said court, grant you this warrant. You are to obey the orders which you shall from time to time receive from the said court, and execute the duties of marshal with fidelity, according to the laws and regulations established for the government and discipline of the militia aforesaid. Given under my hand and seal, at ...., this ...... of ...., A. D., 18..

.... } *President of the Court.*

N. B. With slight alteration, the above form may be used for appointing a marshal for a brigade court-martial for trial of delinquencies.

(No. 27.)

FORM OF SUBPŒNA TO TESTIFY BEFORE A COURT-MARTIAL.

To ....

You are hereby commanded, in the name of the People of the State of New York, personally to be and appear before a (division or brigade) court-martial, for the trial of A. B., of the...... regiment, ...brigade of the National Guard of the State of New York, to be held at the ...., on the .... day of ...., at .... o'clock in the ....noon of that day, to testify all you know in the matter depending, and then and there to be tried, between the said People and A. B., on the part of ....; and this do not omit, on pain of fifty dollars.

Witness my hand, this ...... day ...., A. D., 18..

.... } *President of the Court.*

(No. 28.)

FORM OF A WARRANT TO BE ISSUED BY THE PRESIDENT OF A COURT-MARTIAL, TO COMMIT A DISORDERLY PERSON.

To the sheriff of ...., or to any or either of the constables of .... or the marshal attending this court, *Greeting:*

Whereas, at a (division or brigade) court-martial of the ...., this day held at ...., in ...., in pursuance of the militia laws of this state, for the trial of A. B., of the .... regiment of the .... brigade of the ...... division of the National Guard of the State of New York, one............ was in open court guilty of (here state the offense); and whereas, the said court did thereupon adjudge that the said .... should be committed to the jail of the county of ...., there to remain, without

bail or mainprize, in close confinement, for the space of ....
day.: These are, therefore, in the name of the People of the State
of New York, and by virtue of the said law, to command you forthwith to take the said ...., and convey him
to the jail of the said county of ....; and the
sheriff or jailer of said county is hereby empowered and required to
receive the body of the said ...., and him safely
keep, without bail or mainprize, in close confinement, for the space
of .... day.., and until his fees and the fees of the said
jailer shall be paid, or until he shall be discharged by due course
of law.

Given under my hand and seal, in open court, this .... day
of ...., A. D., 18..

...., *President of the said Court.*

INDEX.

REFERENCE IS MADE TO THE SECTIONS OF THE ACT.

A.

	Section.
Accounts, military, how audited,	39
Adjutant-general, his rank,	98
" " how appointed, and for what time,	51
" " his department,	98
" " to prescribe form of enlisting orders,	162
" " to promulgate orders,	306
" " to keep roster,	254
" " to keep correct descriptions of military districts,	255
" " rosters to be furnished to him by commandants,	257
" " books to be furnished to him by state,	257
" " to have an official seal,	258
" " to cause militia laws to be published,	259
" " enrollment of militia to be filed in his office,	4
" " numbers of regiments, &c., to be registered in his office,	41
" " supernumerary officers to report to him,	46
" " to certify as to numbers,	119
" " to certify as to organization of regiments,	183
" " resignations of certain officers to be transmitted to him,	82
" " his compensation in time of peace,	175
" " his compensation in time of war,	176
" " assistant, his rank and duties,	260
" " " his compensation,	175, 176
Adjutant, regimental,	98
Appeals from election,	70
Appeals, procedure upon,	71
Appeal to commander-in-chief,	72, 202
Appeals from elections, rules for their government,	73
Appeals from decision of court-martial,	213, 243, 244, 245
Appointment of officers in time of war,	84
" " necessary to complete organizations,	23, 24
Appointment of major-generals and commissary-general,	49
Aids to commander-in-chief,	96
" major-general,	97

96 INDEX.

	Section.
Aids to brigadier-general,	97
Army officers exempt from duty,	1
Armory, when furnished,	119
" expense of, a county charge,	120
" to be provided by supervisors,	120, 121
" to be under charge of commandants of regiments,	122
" uniforms and arms to be kept in,	36, 122
" rules for government of, to be prescribed by commander-in-chief,	120
" duties of inspector-general as to,	119, 121
Arms to be furnished by commissary-general on order of commander-in-chief,	123
" not to be furnished until armory is erected or rented,	124
" commandants responsible for safe keeping of,	124
" how distributed to regiments,	125
" how distributed to companies,	129
" bonds for safe keeping of, to be given,	124
" penalty for willful injury to,	130
" to be examined,	131
" distribution of,	302
Appropriation for military purposes,	305
Assessors, their duties,	5
Assessment rolls, commandants to have access to,	5
Articles of war, and army regulations in force in certain cases,	253
Assistant commissary-general, his duties,	104
Assistant inspector-general, his duties,	99
Assistant commissaries of subsistence,	102
Artillery, batteries of, authorized,	31

B.

Brigades, how composed,	30
Battalions, batteries, &c., how organized,	31
Books to be provided,	40
Bands, how organized,	112
Band, leader how appointed,	112
Band, may be disbanded,	117
Brigadier-general to publish orders,	149
Brigadier-generals to attend inspection,	153
Brigade inspector, duties of,	156, 157, 158
Brigadier-general to convene board of auditors,	185
Board of auditors, powers and duties of,	186
" " pay of members,	187
" " to keep records of their proceedings,	187
Brigadier-general, court for trial of,	192
Brevet colonelcy, after twenty years' service,	317
Brigadier-general, how elected,	57, 58
" " appointed in certain cases,	23
" " compensation of,	174
" " to furnish roster to adjutant-general,	256
Brigades to be numbered,	41
Brigades, how organized,	20

INDEX 97

	Section.
Brigade inspectors, how chosen,	53
" " rank and duties of, 98, 156, 157,	158
" " report to be made to,	155
" " compensation of,	174

C.

Camp equipage,	132
Camp of instruction,	165
" " pay for attendance at,	174
Cavalry, extra pay for,	174
Company officers to prepare pay rolls,	178
Clerks of towns and cities, their duties,	5
Commandants of companies to file roster,	13
County treasurer to borrow money on the credit of the county,	15
Company organizations, minimum and maximum,	20
Company officers,	28
Companies to be formed in separate districts,	29
Companies now existing to be deemed organized under this act,	43
Commissary-general, how appointed, 49,	50
" " his oath,	52
Commissions to be issued by commander-in-chief,	74
Certificate of oath indorsed on commission,	76
Companies, special meetings of,	80
Challenges,	88
Commissions to be delivered in 30 days,	90
Commissary of subsistence, his rank and how appointed,	102
Commissaries' assistant,	102
Commissary-general of ordnance, his rank,	104
" " " his duties, 261,	262
Chaplains, qualifications of,	106
Commissary-sergeants,	108
Commissary-general to furnish arms,	123
" " assistant, his rank and duties,	104
Commander-in-chief to superintend enrollment,	4
" " to prescribe rules for armories,	128
" " to order arms to be furnished when necessary,	123
" " to approve bonds for safe keeping of arms,	124
" " to organize militia,	20
" " to appoint officers necessary to facilitate organization,	23
" " may order drafts, 27,	283
" " may organize batteries, &c.,	31
" " may prescribe uniform,	55
" " may direct uniforms to be made,	38
" " may direct books to be furnished,	40
" " shall cause companies, &c., to be numbered,	41
" " shall order elections in certain cases, 44, 57,	85
" " shall nominate major-generals and commissary-general,	49
" " shall appoint his staff,	51
" " shall decide appeals from elections, 70, 72,	73
" " shall issue commissions,	74

13

INDEX.

		Section.
Commander-in-chief shall appoint to fill vacancies in certain cases,		85, 92
" " shall appoint examining board,		91
" " shall appoint retiring board,		94
" " shall have power to suspend in certain cases,		95
" " shall have three aids,		96
" " shall organize staff departments,		110
" " may order parades and drills,		164, 134
" " may order camp of instruction,		165
" " may order lake and sea coast defense duty,		167
" " may designate commandants, &c., of camps and posts,		168
" " shall draw his warrant for expenses of camps, &c.,		172
" " pay of his staff,		175, 176
" " to draw warrant for pay,		180
" " to prescribe rules and forms as to pay,		182
" " appeals to, from court-martial,		202
" " may order national guards into service in certain cases,		284
" " to prescribe rules for distribution of arms,		302
" " may direct upon whom command shall devolve,		303
" " may establish and amend general regulations,		306
Commissary-general to cause arms to be examined,		131
" " to furnish ordnance,		169
" " to sell damaged munitions, &c.,		262
" " to report to commander-in-chief,		263
" " to furnish colors, bugles, &c.,		264
" " to furnish ammunition,		265, 266
" " to make annual report,		267
" " to keep just and true accounts,		268
Companies may form by-laws,		160
Company by-laws, penalty for violation of,		161
Camp of instruction,		165
" " how governed,		166
Camps and posts, commandants how designated,		168
County treasurer to report amount of funds,		188
" " to pay to comptroller $1 for each delinquent,		15
" " to borrow money on credit of county,		15
Courts of inquiry,		189
" " their duties, &c.,		189, 190
" " to whom to report,		190
Courts-martial, for trial of major-general,		191
" " for trial of brigadier-general,		192
" " how ordered and of whom to consist,		193
" " charges and specifications to be served,		194
" " list of officers detailed for, to be served,		194
" " vacancies in, how supplied,		195
" " challenges,		196
" " members to be sworn,		197
" " proceedings of, to be kept by judge-advocate,		198
" " sentence of,		199
" " proceedings of, to be delivered to officer ordering court,		200
" " sentence not to be executed until expiration of time of appeal,		200

INDEX. 99

	Section.
Courts-martial, proceedings and sentence to be transmitted to adjutant-general,	201
" " appeals from, to commander-in-chief,	202
" " compensation of members of,	203, 204
" " regimental,	205
" " " appointment of, to be published,	206
" " " may collect company fines,	252
" " " vacancies, how filled,	207
" " " oath, how taken,	208, 209
" " " delinquents, how summoned to,	210
" " " return of delinquents,	211
" " " powers of,	212
" " " appeal from decision of,	213
" " " compensation of members of,	214
" " " fines and penalties to be paid county treasurer,	215
" " president and judge-advocate to issue subpœnas,	232
" " presidents of, have power to administer oaths,	233
" " " may excuse for cause,	222
" " may compel attendance of witnesses,	234
" " penalty for non-attendance as a witness at,	236
" " may issue attachment against witnesses,	235
" " attachment issued by, how executed,	236
" " disorderly conduct at, how punished,	237
" " warrant issued by, form of,	238
" " sheriff to receive body of person committed by,	239
" " president being absent, senior officer to preside,	240
" " members of, to sit in full uniform,	240
" " president of, to appoint marshal,	241
" " powers and duties of marshals of,	242
" " statement of, to be furnished officer hearing appeal,	243
" " further evidence may be taken on appeal from,	244
" " when composed of one person he shall be president,	249
" " presidents of, to prosecute delinquent sheriffs, &c.,	248
" " delinquent officers to be returned to, by chiefs of staff,	250
" " for trial of officers absent from parade, how composed,	250
" " course of procedure,	250
" " may excuse delinquents,	251
" " articles of war to govern in certain cases,	253
Company drills,	136
Colonelcy by brevet,	317
Colonel, pay of,	174
" appointed in certain cases,	23
Costs, security for, in certain cases,	224
Companies, organization of,	20, 28, 31
" to be numbered,	41
" to receive volunteers,	26
" when to be deemed organized,	26
Company districts to remain as at present,	20
" how altered,	20
Companies to be filled by draft in certain cases,	27, 298
Colonels to appoint non-commissioned officers in certain cases,	24

	Section.
Corporals, number of, to company,	28
Company officers,	28
Companies of cavalry and artillery, organization of,	28
Colonels, how appointed,	23
" how elected,	59
Company officers, how appointed,	25
Company officers, how elected,	53, 60
Certificate of service,	307
" of membership,	308
Collector, duty of,	14
County treasurer to pay certain moneys to comptroller,	12
County treasurers, their powers and duties,	15

D.

Districts, how altered, consolidated, &c.,	20
Drafts,	27, 283, 298, 299, 300, 301
Drum majors,	108
Drills of officers and non-commissioned officers,	151
Division inspectors, reports to be made to,	157
Division parades,	163
Delinquents,	14
District attorney to prosecute in certain cases,	295
Discipline and exercise,	25
Divisions, how organized,	20, 21
" number of,	21
" of how many brigades to consist,	30
" review of,	152
Division districts to remain organized as at present,	20
" " how altered,	20
" " to be numbered, &c.,	41
Drills, company,	136
Drills, officers,	151
Division commandant, of his duties, &c.,	163
Deficiency, how raised by supervisors,	18

E.

Exemptions,	1, 3, 10, 11
" how proven,	8
Enrollment, how made,	4
" notice of, how published,	8
" duties of assessors in respect to,	5
" duties of tavern keepers in respect to,	6
" duties of clerks of towns and cities in respect to,	5
" false information in respect to, how punished,	7
" to be copied and filed,	8
Election of brigadier-general and brigade-inspector, notice of, how served,	45, 58
" for field officers, when held,	44
" to fill vacancy in field officer,	59

INDEX. 101

	Section.
Election to fill vacancy of captain or subaltern,	60
" notice of, how served,	61, 62, 63
" how conducted,	64
" presiding officer at,	65
" polls at,	66
" canvass of votes,	66
" certificate of,	67
" vacancy caused by, how filled,	68
" appeal from,	70, 71
" of non-commissioned officers, how conducted,	79, 80, 81
" to fill vacancy,	85
" challenges at,	88
" oath of voter at,	89
" for officers rejected by examining board,	91
" parades not to be made within five days of,	137
Engineer-in-chief,	100
" division,	100
" brigade,	100
" regimental,	100

F.

False information, giving of, how punished,	7
Firemen not to be included in enrollment,	9
Foremen of fire companies to file lists of members,	9
Fine for non-attendance at drill of reserve militia,	14
Fine, how collected,	14, 15, 16, 17, 18
Fire-arms, unlawful discharge of, how punished,	220
Fantastical dress, wearing of, how punished,	221
Fines, how collected,	225
" imprisonment for non-payment of,	225
" duty of jailer if not paid,	226
" warrant for collection of, may be executed in all parts of state,	227
" warrant for collection of, may be renewed,	228, 229, 247
" to be paid into county treasury,	230
" bonds for collection of,	231
" company, how collected,	252
Ferries and toll bridges, free passage over,	316

G.

Governor of the State of New York, his acts confirmed, ... 284

H.

Highway tax, exemption from, ... 146

I.

Inspector-general, rank and duties of,	99
Inspector-general assistant,	99
Inspector of military accounts,	99

	Section.
Inspector-general, his duties as to armories, &c.,	119, 121
Inspection, annual,	133
Inspector-general to be notified of encampments, &c.,	149
Inspection, duties of commandants of companies,	154
Inspection, duties of commandants of regiments,	155
Inspector, brigade, duties of,	156, 157, 158
Inspector, division, return to be made to,	157
Inspector, division, to report to inspector-general,	276
Inspection to be attended by brigadier-generals,	153
Inspection, absence of general officers and staff from, how punished,	159
Inquiry, courts of, their duties, &c.,	189, 190
Ignorance or neglect of duty, how punished,	216
Inspector-general, his duties,	271
" " to report as to missing and damaged arms,	272
" " to inspect camp equipage,	273
" " to report as to encampments,	274
" " matters at a distance to be referred to him,	275
" " questions as to qualifications of officers referred to him,	275
" " division and brigade inspectors to report to him,	276
" " shall visit camps,	277
" " shall examine books and accounts of auditing boards,	278
Invasion, duty of commandants in case of,	285
Invasion, notice of, to be given commander-in-chief,	287
Insurrection, notice of, to be given to county judge,	288
" duty of county judge in case of,	289
" persons wounded in opposing, to be provided for,	290
" notice of, to be given to commandant of brigade and commander-in-chief,	287

J.

Judge-advocate-general, his rank,	106
" " " his duties,	269, 280, 281
" " " the legal adviser of the departments,	281
" " " his compensation,	175, 176
Judge-advocates, division and brigade,	106
Judge-advocates to keep proceedings of courts-martial secret,	198
Judge-advocates to attend courts of inquiry,	189
" " compensation of,	203
Judge-advocate-general's department officers may be detailed to other duty,	282
Jury duty, exemption from,	146

K.

Keepers o taverns, their duties as to enrollments,	6

L.

Light artillery and light infantry, organization of,	22
Lake and sea coast defense duty,	167

INDEX. 103

M.

	Section.
Militia, present uniformed, to form part of national guard,	22
Minors not to enlist without consent of parents,	33
Minors may be drafted,	1, 27, 33
Militia reserve, 1st and 2d classes,	12
Militia reserve, general parade of,	13
Major-general, how appointed,	49, 50
Military secretary,	91
Musicians, duties of,	113
" returns of delinquents,	115
Major-general to review brigades of his division,	152
Major-general, powers and duties of,	163
" " court-martial for trial of,	191
Money, refusal to pay over, how punished,	217
Mayors of cities may call for military aid in case of riot,	291
Military fund, regimental,	183
Military fund of state,	304
Military purposes, appropriation for,	305

N.

National Guard of the State of New York,	21
" " limited to 30,000 in time of peace,	27
" " companies to be formed in separate districts,	29
" " divisions, how composed,	30
" " brigades, how composed,	30
" " regiments,	30
" " battalions, batteries, &c.,	31
Non-commissioned officers, how appointed,	24, 53, 56
" " " warnings to,	138
" " " length of service,	146
" " " privileges of,	146
" " " compensation of,	174
Notices of election of field officers, how served,	59
" " captains and subalterns,	60

O.

Organization,	20, 25, 26
Officers, commissioned, in what cases appointed,	23
Officers, non-commissioned, in what cases appointed,	24
Officers, company,	28
Officers, how commissioned and removed,	55
Officers, non-commissioned, how appointed and removed,	56
Officers elected, names to be sent to commander-in-chief,	69
Oath of commissioned officers,	75
Oath, certificate of, indorsed on commission,	76
" no fee for administering,	76
Officers, service of notices upon,	148
Orders for encampment and inspection, how published,	149
Orders may be read at parades, &c.,	149
Orders, disobedience of, how punished,	216

INDEX.

	Section.
Ordnance sergeants to be keepers of armories,	311
Ordnance, commissary-general of,	52

P.

Parade of reserve militia,	13
Penalty in case certain officers do not perform duties as to enrollment,	19
Poll lists, commandants to have access to,	5
Penalty for refusing information as to enrollment,	7
Penalty if uniform be removed or secreted,	37
Paymaster-general, his rank,	103
Paymaster, division and brigade,	103
Paymasters, may be detached,	103
Parades and drills, number of,	134
" " " how ordered,	134
" " " power of commanding officer,	135
Pay of forces in time of war,	173
Pay of forces at camps and posts,	174
Pay of staff of commander-in-chief in time of peace,	175
Pay of staff of commander-in-chief in time of war,	176
Pay of clerks in staff departments,	177
" roll, non-commissioned officers and privates,	178
" " " officers,	179
Pay, commander-in-chief to draw warrant for,	180
Paymaster-general or other paymaster to make payments,	181
Pay, rules as to, commander-in-chief to prescribe,	182
Pay of members of regimental boards,	187
Penalties,	216, 217, 218, 219, 220, 221
Penalty for refusal to deliver state property,	313
Pay of forces called out to suppress riots,	318

Q.

Quartermaster-general, his rank,	101
Quartermasters, division, brigade, regimental,	101
Quartermaster-general to cause uniforms to be made,	38
Quartermaster-sergeants,	108
Quartermaster-general to furnish camp equipage, &c.,	170

R.

Reserve militia, first and second classes,	12
Regiments, how composed,	30
Residence, change of, not to vacate office,	48
Resignations, how made,	82, 83, 84
Removal from bounds of command,	86
Retiring board,	93, 94
Returns, how made,	140
" to whom delivered,	141
" to be evidence,	142
" of delinquencies of non-commissioned officers,	143
Regimental fund, how composed,	183

INDEX.

	Section.
Regimental board of auditors,	184
" board, powers and duties of,	186
" board to keep record of proceedings,	187
Rendezvous for actual service, punishment for failure to attend,	218
Return, false, how punished,	218
Reserve militia to be drafted, in what cases,	283
Riot, duty of sheriff or mayor,	291
Riot, in case of, forces to be furnished with ammunition,	293
" " penalty for neglect of duty,	294, 296
" " penalty to be enforced by district attorney,	297
" " those injured to be provided for,	297
Rules and regulations to be published,	306
Repeal of inconsistent acts,	319
Roster to be kept by adjutant-general,	254
Revised Statutes, certain provisions of to apply to this act,	16

S.

Substitutes,	27
Supervisors to raise money by taxation,	15
" penalty, in case they refuse to act,	19
Supernumerary officers,	46
Staff of commander-in-chief,	51
Staffs of major and brigadier-generals,	97
Staff officers, how appointed,	54
Suspension of officers from command,	95
Storekeepers,	101, 104
Surgeon-general, his rank, &c.,	105
Surgeons of division, brigade and regiment,	105
" mates,	105
" qualifications of,	105
Sergeant standard-bearers,	108
" majors,	108
" quartermaster,	108
" commissary,	108
" ordnance,	311
Sheriff, his powers in case of riot,	291
State property, penalty for refusal to deliver,	314
" " illegally detained, may be taken possession of,	314
Supervisors to furnish armories,	120, 121

T.

Tavernkeepers, duties of, as to enrollment,	6
Time of service, how computed,	2
Trumpet-majors,	108
Taxes, exemption from,	146

U.

Uniformed militia not to be enrolled,	9
" " to be included in national guard,	22
Uniforms, when furnished by state,	35

	Section.
Uniforms, to be kept at armory,	36
" neglect to provide, how punished,	216
Uniform,	34

V.

Volunteers, how received,	47
Vacancy of brigadier-general, how filled,	57
" caused by election, how filled,	68
Votes necessary to a choice,	81
Vacancies, how filled,	85
Voters, their qualifications,	87
Voter, oath of,	89
Vacancy, member of court-martial,	195
Violation of company by-laws, penalty for,	161

W.

Warnings to attend parade, how issued and served,	138, 139, 147, 148
" without warrant, when,	144
Warrant, form of, for arrest of disorderly persons,	238
Warrant for collection of fines,	225
" " renewal of,	226
Warrant appointing marshal,	241

AN ACT

TO ENFORCE THE LAWS AND PRESERVE ORDER.

Passed April 15, 1845.

[Published in accordance with provisions of Militia Law of April 23, 1862.]

The People of the State of New York, represented in Senate and Assembly, do enact as follows:

§ 1. The commander-in-chief may, on the application of any sheriff, deputy sheriff or district attorney, or either of them, or of the mayor or recorder of any city, or of the commander of any uniform company, loan to such officer, or to any military company, or to any number of citizens, or to any city, village or town, any number of stands of arms and military equipage, from any of the arsenals or military stores of this state, which he shall deem proper, and for such time and on such terms and conditions and security as he shall deem proper. *Arms, &c., may be loaned in certain cases.*

§ 2. On the application of the sheriff, under sheriff or district attorney of any county of this state, with the assent of a majority of the judges of the county courts of such county, the governor may, if in his opinion it shall be necessary and proper, authorize such sheriff, under sheriff, district attorney, or some deputy sheriff, to contract with and organize a guard for the protection of any jail or prison in said county, or to arrest, detain, or have in safe keeping any prisoner or prisoners, or to enforce any process, judgment or decree of any court; which application and authority shall be in writing, and a copy thereof filed and recorded in the office of the secretary of state. *Guard to protect jail may be organized.*

§ 3. The said written authority shall specify the number of persons beyond which the said guard shall not extend. *Number.*

§ 4. The governor may at any time revoke, alter or modify such authority. *Revocation.*

§ 5. The governor may, in his discretion, permit such sheriff, under sheriff or deputy to contract with any uniform company or companies to form such guard. *Contract may be made with guard.*

§ 6. Such guard, when so formed, shall be under the command and direction of such officer or officers as shall be designated by the governor, and in case he shall not make such designation, then under the command of the sheriff, under sheriff or deputy, and of such officer or officers, military or civil, as shall be designated by such sheriff or deputy; and shall be subject to all such rules and regulations for their government and action as shall have been *Guard, how to be commanded.*

agreed on at the time of their organization, or afterwards directed by the governor; and the governor may deliver to such guard any amount of ammunition or cartridges that he shall think proper and necessary.

Penalties. § 7. The members of the said guard shall be subject to such penalties and forfeitures, for neglect of duty or disobedience of orders, as shall have been prescribed at the time of their organization, or afterwards, by the governor.

Per diem allowance. § 8. Such guard shall receive, as a compensation for their services, such per diem allowance as shall have been agreed upon at the time of their employment, or at any time afterwards, not exceeding, however, the sum of one dollar per day for each private, and for each officer such sum as shall have been agreed on, not exceeding two dollars per day.

Vouchers as to performance of service. § 9. The comptroller may require such vouchers and proofs of the agreements and performance of service under this act as he shall deem proper, and shall from time to time audit and allow the accounts therefor as he shall deem just; and when so audited and allowed, shall draw his warrant on the treasurer for the payment thereof, and the treasurer shall pay the same out of any moneys not otherwise appropriated.

In relation to expenses § 10. The comptroller may require such vouchers and proofs, in relation to all and each of any such expenses, as he shall deem proper.

Money paid to be charged to county. § 11. All moneys paid from the treasury on the warrant of the comptroller, by virtue of any of the foregoing provisions of this act, shall be charged by the comptroller to the county for whose benefit the same has been so paid, and he shall certify the amount thereof to the treasurer of said county.

Duty of county treasurer. § 12. It shall be the duty of such county treasurer to lay the same before the supervisors of said county at their next annual meeting.

Duty of supervisors. § 13. The said supervisors shall, at their next annual meeting, cause the amount thereof to be levied and collected as other county charges are now by law directed to be levied: Provided, however, if the said board of supervisors shall think it would be unreasonably burthensome to such county to raise the whole thereof in one year, the said sum so to be raised may be divided into two or three equal parts, one whereof shall be levied and collected in each succeeding year, until the whole sum shall be so levied and collected.

Money to be paid into state treasury. § 14. The sum or sums levied by virtue of the last preceding section shall be paid over to the county treasurer, who shall, on or before the first day of May thereafter, pay over the same to the treasurer of the state, to the credit of such county.

Temporary guard. § 15. Whenever the sheriff of any county shall deem it necessary to raise a temporary guard for the protection of a jail or prison, or the safe keeping of prisoners, he may, with the assent of one of the judges of the county courts, employ such temporary guard as may be necessary until a guard can with reasonable diligence be formed and organized under the second section of this act; the expenses of which said temporary guard shall be audited, allowed and paid by the board of supervisors of said county, as other county charges.

§ 16. The expenses of the sheriff or other county officer, incurred in pursuance of any of the provisions of this act, shall be audited, allowed and paid by the board of supervisors of the county, and shall be a portion of the county charges of such county, to be levied and raised as other county charges are by law levied and paid. *Expense, how paid.*

§ 17. Every person who shall resist or enter into a combination with any person or persons to resist the execution of process, shall be guilty of a misdemeanor, and be punished by imprisonment in the county jail for a term not exceeding one year, or by a fine not exceeding one thousand dollars, or by both such fine and imprisonment, in the discretion of the court. *Penalty for resisting execution of process.*

§ 18. Section eighty, in article seven of title six, of chapter seven of the third part of the Revised Statutes, is hereby amended, so that the said section shall read: "Whenever a sheriff or other public officer, authorized to execute any process delivered to him, shall find or have reason to apprehend that resistance will be made to the execution of such process, he shall be authorized to command every male inhabitant of his county, or as many as he shall think proper, and with such arms as he shall direct, and any military company or companies in said county, armed and equipped, to assist him in overcoming such resistance, and, if necessary, in seizing, arresting and confining the resisters, their aiders and abettors, to be dealt with according to law." *Revised Statutes amended. Power of sheriff to call out inhabitants.*

§ 19. Whenever the governor shall be satisfied that the execution of civil or criminal process has been forcibly resisted in any county or counties of this state, by bodies of men, or that combinations to resist the execution of such process by force exist in any such county or counties, and that the power of such county or counties has been exerted and is not sufficient to enable the officer having such process to execute the same, he may, on the application of such officer or of the district attorney of such county, or of one of the judges of the county courts thereof, by proclamation to be published in the state paper, and in such other papers as he shall direct, declare such county or counties to be in a state of insurrection; and may order into the service of the state such number and description of volunteer or uniform companies or other militia of this state as he shall deem necessary, to serve for such term as he shall direct, and under the command of such officer or officers as he shall think proper; and the governor may, when he *County, when to be declared in a state of insurrection. Volunteer companies may be ordered into service.*

shall think proper, revoke, or declare that such proclamation shall cease at such time and in such manner as he shall direct.

Penalty for resisting execution of process. § 20. Any person or persons who shall, after the publication of such proclamation by the governor, as provided in section nineteen of this act, resist or assist in resisting the execution of any process in any such county so declared to be in a state of insurrection, or who shall aid or attempt the rescue or escape of any prisoner from lawful custody or confinement, or who shall resist, or aid or assist in resisting any force ordered out by the governor to quell or suppress any such insurrection, shall, upon conviction, be adjudged guilty of a felony, and punished by imprisonment in the state prison for a term not less than two years.

Militia called into service, how paid. § 21. Whenever any portion of the militia shall be ordered into service by the governor, in pursuance of section nineteen of this act, they shall be paid therefor at the following rates, to wit: To each private the sum of one dollar per day; to each non-commissioned officer and musician the sum of one dollar and twenty-five cents per day; and to all commissioned officers of the line, and to the field and staff officers, the same compensation as is paid to officers of the army in the service of the United States, together with all necessary rations and forage, and for the horses of any mounted men one dollar per day.

Expenses under sections 19 and 21, how paid. § 22. The expenses under the sections nineteen and twenty-one, and also of the commissariat and other military departments, shall be audited and allowed by the comptroller, and on his warrant paid by the treasurer out of any money in the treasury not otherwise appropriated.

§ 23. This act shall take effect immediately.

www.ingramcontent.com/pod-product-compliance
Lightning Source LLC
Chambersburg PA
CBHW020146170426
43199CB00010B/910